The
PREGNANT
Woman's
COMPANION

Library of Congress Cataloging-in-Publication Data

D'Amico, Christine
    The pregnant woman's companion : nine strategies that work to keep your peace of mind through pregnancy and into parenthood / by Chrisine D'Amico with contributions from Margaret Taylor. — 1st ed.
    p. cm.
    Includes bibliographical references and index.
    LCCN 2002090310
    ISBN 0-9716631-0-6

    1. Pregnancy — Psychological aspects. 2. Pregnant women — Psychology. 3. Pregnancy — Popular works. I. Taylor, Margaret (Margaret A.), 1946- II. Title.

RG560.D36 2002   618.2'4'019
                                  QB102-200142

The PREGNANT *Woman's* COMPANION

Christine D'Amico, MA
with
Margaret A. Taylor, MS, CNM

Photographs by Bill Cameron, Christine D'Amico,
and a collection of really creative moms!

Book Design by Polly Lockman

ATTITUDE press, Inc.
Minneapolis, Minnesota

This book is dedicated to babies, pregnant women, their partners and caregivers throughout the ages. Regardless of your circumstances, challenges and outcomes, you are participating in a true miracle here on earth.

Table of Contents

Acknowledgements

Writing this book has been an amazing and lengthy journey, and along the way there have been contributions from many wise and caring individuals.

Thank you to the founders of CTI, Cynthia, and Julia, the coaches that helped me find my way back to writing.

My warmest gratitude goes out to the new parents, pregnant women and their partners who were willing to share photographs of themselves and their beautiful babies, welcome me into their lives, and pass along their stories. Without their willingness, honesty and clear expression, this book could not exist.

This project has been truly blessed by the contributions of Margaret Taylor. Her expertise on caring for pregnant women and birthing babies was invaluable, her passion for women finding their strength and living self-directed lives was inspiring, and her personal insight into the true emotion of what it means to live through a major life transition was humbling. Margaret, you are a blessing to every life you touch!

To my agent Andrea Pedolsky — what can I say? — Your wisdom, savvy and pure New York-book-know-how made this book a resource that has the potential to be so much for so many. You could see the forest I was trying to build with the jumbled clump of trees I presented. Thank you for taking a risk on me. With some hard work and a bit of luck, I plan to ensure that you see it pay off.

Finally, thanks to my family: husband, fathers, mothers, aunts, grandparents and sons. I could ask for no better loved ones in my life. Throughout my journey, each of you has provided support and encouragement in unique and beautiful ways. With support and love like this, "impossible" things can happen everyday!

A Welcome From Margaret

Pregnancy is forty weeks long, give or take two weeks. That relatively brief span of days has a powerful impact on the individuals involved. It is a challenging time in the life of a pregnant woman and her partner, filled with new thoughts, feelings and behaviors. All of the physical and biological changes occurring simultaneously with the new realization of impending awesome responsibilities can produce anxiety and stress. For instance, coping with constant nausea coupled with the excitement of pregnancy confirmation . . . watching your abdomen expand while feeling the first delicate movements of the baby growing within you . . .dealing with family obligations while challenged by the aches, pains and exhaustion of pregnancy. These evolving situations are just a few of the concerns I hear women and couples express during prenatal visits.

If I had all the time in the world, I would help the pregnant woman and her partner focus on the specific issues they are facing, identify their options and choices, and support them in the action they decide to take. I then would follow up with them via a phone call to see how things are going. But with the demands of a full patient schedule, this is just not realistic for most medical practitioners. Our focus is on attending to those physical and biological needs mentioned earlier. However, this kind of personal support is what coaching is all about, and it is what makes this book so useful for pregnant women. Christine and I have taken the principles of coaching and applied them to this very unique and special life event.

Here you have a pregnancy book focused on helping you take action toward the realization of your own visions, goals and desires. A pregnancy book that is part friend, part mentor and one hundred-percent dedicated to encouraging you to listen to your needs and live in accordance with your values. A pregnancy book that asks powerful questions, expands perspectives and openly questions unwanted limitations.

It is not designed to be a "cookbook." It does not provide step-by-step recipes for solving all of your problems. Pregnancy is just not that simple, and each of your unique situations will require a unique solution. However, this book does provide you with an abundance of tools and perspectives that will make navigating this awesome experience called pregnancy much easier.

Whether you are in a first or subsequent pregnancy, we hope this resource will increase your peace of mind through the ins and outs of the experience and that it will further your ability to take the best possible care of yourself and your baby from today on into your life as a parent. Read, reflect, respond and then, most of all, as you journey through your pregnancy, make the most of all the magical life experience it has to offer.

Introduction

When people ask me what I do, I usually answer, "I provide individual coaching to people in transition, which means situations such as career change, retirement or pregnancy." And if the person I'm talking with has been through a pregnancy of her own, her eyes light up at the inclusion of pregnancy as a time of transition, and she overflows with words about how much unexpected life change came with her own pregnancy and early parenting experiences. It seems that in all the flurry surrounding the arrival of a baby, any attention for the shifting lives of the parents is lost, leaving Mom and Dad to stumble along in a thicket of stress and overwhelmed feelings.

My clients and I work with the concept of change everyday — and it is a process with which I am very comfortable — but even with all of my awareness, I was thrown off balance by the twists and turns of my own pregnancy and introduction into parenthood. Out of my personal challenges and the conversations I had with many other pregnant women and their partners, I decided to take what I knew as a life transition coach and apply it to pregnancy. I wanted to create a resource that would make this explosive time of life easier, calmer and more enriching for pregnant women and their partners. Four years later, *The Pregnant Woman's Companion* was ready for publication.

To make the most of this pregnancy resource, it would be helpful to know a bit about personal coaching. Coaching is for people whose lives are basically working and who are looking to deepen, strengthen, clarify or expand what they already have. As a coach, I am not trained to work with people on the more clinical issues of depression, abuse, addiction, or the like. People with these conditions are best served by professionals trained specifically for such life challenges. However, I do have clients who are facing or have faced many of these hurdles and are seeking the guidance of an appropriate professional — and at the same time want to further their lives through the help of a coach.

The Pregnant Woman's Companion follows the same role model. It is written to make life easier and more peaceful for the pregnant woman who is basically finding her way. If, as a pregnant woman, you are facing issues as big as physical or sexual abuse, addiction, or depression, this book can still be a resource to you, but it will likely not be enough. These hurdles are far too daunting and usually require the help of a professional. So, for the sake of yourself and your baby, take action now to get some help.

When done in person, coaching is a process of listening to the client and helping her find her own best solutions. It is stepping away from the idea of one "right" way of doing something and, instead, opening up the options, reaching beyond limitations and helping the client see what she really wants above all else.

As a reader of this book, you have an opportunity to find the same thing in a slightly different form. A common personal challenge of pregnancy is captured in each of the nine strategies that make up this book. Each strategy addresses a multitude of sub-topics and provides an array of vehicles for gaining clarity on your own unique situation by helping you to:

➤ Make decisions that are best for you.

➤ See situations from a different perspective.

➤ Gain support during a challenging time.

➤ Locate the information or resources you need on a specific topic.

➤ Begin doing something that is important to you.

➤ Reassure yourself that you are managing your pregnancy in the best way to meet your needs.

➤ Question some of the discardable assumptions or limitations you have been living with surrounding pregnancy.

➤ Celebrate and honor the miracle in which you are participating.

➤ Step out of your hectic life for a couple of moments to rest and reflect.

➤ Build your relationship with your pregnancy partner.

Through this book, you have countless opportunities to listen to yourself. You have a place to find a whole new perspective. You have more options to consider than any one pregnant woman could actually do in nine months. You have tools for clarifying what you want most, and you have a resource that respects your needs, desires and personal choices.

The goal is to enable you to design your pregnancy process to be the best it can be for you and your pregnancy partner. I encourage you to flip through the book and find what has meaning for you right now. No need to read it front to back! Share this book with your pregnancy partner. Talk with him or her about what stands out for both of you. Use this book to assist you in planning what you really want during these nine months. Call upon The *Pregnant Woman's Companion* to help you walk with courage and authenticity towards the opportunities or challenges that present themselves during your pregnancy.

I know each one of us has a brilliance to share with the world, and coaching is about bringing each client closer and closer to that brilliance. Whether you believe it or not, you have all of the wisdom, resourcefulness and creativity you need to be a strong and extraordinary pregnant woman. May this book allow your unique brilliance to shine as you move through the nine months of your pregnancy and into those first years of parenthood.

Here you are, just beginning. You may be excited, scared, nervous, confident or all of that mixed together. You are warmly welcomed into these pages, wherever you currently are on your pregnancy journey.

THE TRUTH BEHIND YOUR PREGNANT GLOW

Whatever stage of pregnancy you are in, trying to conceive, in your initial weeks, beginning to show, or facing the onset of labor, you know the reality of all this pregnancy stuff is not quite as sweet and romantic as popular culture makes it out to be. Kim was shocked at how her pregnancy experience was so unlike the one she had expected. She describes it like this:

I am 33, and I am pregnant. Being pregnant has presented a whirlwind of new experiences and emotions. Many of them have thrown me for a loop. I went into pregnancy expecting it to be a dreamy time, where my husband and I happily prepared our nest for the arrival of our long-awaited child. I was terribly wrong. At nine weeks, my experience is nothing like my romantic prepregnant image. I have morning sickness, and I feel awful most of the time.

I've read the books, an armful of them. And from them I learned what kinds of food to eat, how much weight to gain and what body changes to expect. I uncovered how to pick a healthcare provider and what kinds of questions to make sure I asked. I learned about all of the medical conditions I could encounter and when to call my healthcare provider with an emergency. But what I didn't find was how to deal with all of the personal change, stress and confusing emotions I am experiencing. This pregnancy has affected every part of my life. So why didn't anyone tell me it would be like this, so hard to keep a grounded perspective? Why don't people talk about the personal and emotional challenges that come with pregnancy?

This is a common beginning for many pregnant women and their partners. The outside world is focused on your pregnant body and your baby. But the effects of pregnancy go far beyond your physical body. You may have to work, eat, sleep or socialize very differently or in ways you do not prefer. To make it all worse, when you try to tell someone about the challenges you are facing, those around you may brush off your experience with a flippant comment like, "Oh, it's all worth it," or even worse, "Don't worry, dear. You won't even remember this once the baby is born." And maybe that is true — but it sure doesn't do anything to help you out now — when it often leaves you feeling off-balance, overwhelmed, way out of your comfort zone or downright confused. Below is a series of questions to get you thinking about where you currently are in your pregnancy:

➤ What is the biggest challenge right now?

➤ Where do you feel your peace of mind eroding around the edges?

➤ In what areas would it be most helpful to bring some relief into your pregnant life?

➤ Where can you see your own resistance getting in your way?

➤ What are the opportunities you have not allowed yourself to notice?

➤ Where do you want some additional support?

Nine Simple Strategies

The goal of this book is to equip you with nine strategies for keeping your peace of mind and personal power as you traverse some of the unexpected personal challenges, new transitions and strong emotions you may experience throughout your pregnancy. These strategies speak to the nonmedical issues that often cause the most chaos for pregnant women and their partners. Putting these nine strategies to work in your pregnancy can help you bring calm into any pregnancy situation, smooth out many of the bumps, increase your sense of personal peace of mind and free you up to fully enjoy this miraculous nine-month adventure.

So think about the most recent event in your pregnancy that left you rolling your eyes and wondering how in the world you would survive it, and then read the descriptions below to see which of the nine strategies could be of most assistance.

STRATEGY ONE: GIVE YOURSELF THE BEST BY CREATING AND CALLING UPON A COMMITTED SUPPORT SYSTEM.

This sounds pretty straightforward: get some help, no big deal. But it is often one of the biggest challenges you can face, and doing it well can make all the difference in keeping your peace of mind throughout pregnancy. The specifics outlined in this strategy will help you design your best support system, both in terms of a committed pregnancy partner as well as a larger community of support. You will also learn how to remove some of your own blocks to getting support, so you can have the support you want right away. You do not have to feel alone or isolated within your pregnancy experience.

STRATEGY TWO: ALLOW YOURSELF TO LET GO OF SOCIAL STANDARDS AND CREATE A NEW RELATIONSHIP WITH YOUR BODY.

So much about your body is changing constantly throughout your pregnancy. This strategy shifts your focus away from the specific details of these bodily changes and towards, how you personally go about balancing all of the twists and turns your body is making. In applying this strategy to your pregnancy, you will gain additional respect for your body and the amazing things it can do, find some new ways to make peace with this beautiful body you have been given, and further let go of the unrealistic social standards constraining women and their bodies. Finally, this strategy provides added support to women whose challenges with their bodies include more dramatic physical limitations such as morning sickness or bedrest.

STRATEGY THREE: PARE DOWN COMMITMENTS TO A LIMITED SET OF LIFE PRIORITIES.

For many of us, life was much too busy before we were pregnant. And now, adding to that schedule all the demands of a pregnancy can leave your head spinning. This strategy calls you to stop and reassess what you will continue doing and what you must release. Here you will decide what matters most, and then make the changes needed to reduce your load of commitments before they send you reeling. The strategy is designed to help you simplify what you have committed to in life so you have the time to enjoy all of the beautiful moments of pregnancy, as well as to get yourself prepared for parenthood. This nine-month experience is far too amazing and brief to be lost in stressed time schedules and over-committed social calendars.

STRATEGY FOUR: EASE YOUR WAY INTO PARENTHOOD DURING YOUR NINE MONTHS OF PREGNANCY.

Now that you have used the previous strategy to clear out some of the clutter, you have the time to consciously take some initial steps into the awesome role of parent. Whether you take time to notice its arrival or not, you begin metamorphosing into a parent throughout your nine months of pregnancy. This strategy assists you in getting prepared to become the best parent you can be by guiding you through some of your first major parenting decisions. In applying this strategy you will look at your current work and career through the lens of a parent, begin the process of working through an initial balance between work and family, and explore how parenthood will affect many of your other roles in life. This strategy aids you in laying a solid foundation from which to step into parenthood, one of the most challenging and rewarding aspects of your life.

STRATEGY FIVE: CALL UPON YOUR INTERNAL STRENGTHS WHEN FACING A SITUATION YOU CANNOT CONTROL.

As you may already know, pregnancy is an experience filled with a great deal you cannot control. Is the baby okay? Will I miscarry? Is the fetus forming correctly? You can get good information on a lot of these and other related questions, but there are some questions you simply cannot answer. You need to wait and let the process unfold. Waiting with unknowns is hard in the best of situations, but it is almost impossible when it is about the well-being of your unborn baby. Waiting, worrying and fearing the unknown can make you crazy on and off throughout your pregnancy. This strategy should help you create some peace and comfort for yourself amidst all of this turbulence by reconnecting you with three of your own internal strengths, each of which can make it much easier to accept the situation you must live with, calm your fears and provide you with some needed reassurance.

STRATEGY SIX: WATCH FOR OPPORTUNITIES TO BALANCE THE UPS AND DOWNS OF FAMILY LIFE.

For most people, family interactions come with a combination of positive and negative charges. Many of these charges are the remnants of the good and bad experiences from the family in which you were raised. Now you are innocently creating your own family, but all of your past positive and negative family experiences are also coming along for the ride. This strategy reminds you to attend to your past experiences of family so they work to your benefit and don't get in the way of your pregnancy, your future family experiences or the well-being of this tender new family you will be building in the years to come. This strategy will call on you to indulge in the budding images of what you want to create with your new family, to turn and face any familial skeletons that may be hanging in your own closet and, finally, to welcome you into this powerful institution called family, a building block of many aspects of our society.

STRATEGY SEVEN: MAKE NEW FRIENDS AND CONSCIOUSLY CHOOSE WHAT YOU WANT TO DO WITH THE OLD.

Pregnancy is a normal time for friendships to do some shifting around. You are going through so many changes and building a new set of interests, it just makes sense that your friendships will end up looking different than they did prior to your pregnancy. It can be easy to forget this when your focus is on the arrival of your baby. This strategy opens up your awareness so the coming changes in your friendships don't cause you or your friends confusion, discomfort, stress, misunderstanding or hurt feelings. By setting your expectations in alignment with this strategy, you will be clearer and more comfortable when balancing the push and pull of your friendships. Some of the specific assistance included in this strategy covers how to maintain your connection to those friends who are important to you, letting go of others in a caring way and opening yourself to find the new friendships you crave. Taking advantage of the ideas in this strategy will keep you from getting stuck in an ill-fitting routine with friends.

STRATEGY EIGHT: FIND YOUR WAY TO GENTLENESS WITH YOUR SPOUSE.

In both pregnant and nonpregnant life, when the going gets tough, the tough often take it out on their spouses. Unfortunately, as you know, if you've ever responded this way to stress, it only adds to your list of discomforts. This strategy for keeping your peace of mind through pregnancy focuses on how you and your spouse can build some new understandings and spend the nine months of pregnancy supporting and caring for one another rather than bickering or fighting your way through the experience. Some ways this strategy can help you is by providing you with an exercise to keep the mundane details of life from getting in the way of your serenity, increasing the comfort with your growing interdependence upon one another and, finally, opening up a conversation about the expectations you hold regarding romantic love during pregnancy.

STRATEGY NINE: LIGHTEN YOUR LOAD BY FACING YOUR PREGNANCY LOSSES.

Hopefully, your pregnancy will not contain a painful loss, but, unfortunately, loss is oftentimes a part of pregnancy and a challenge pregnant women and their partners may have to face. Pregnancy losses can take many forms. Some are dramatic and obvious to the world, such as a stillborn baby while others are silent and painfully personal such as a miscarriage or a labor process that did not go as planned. Whether the loss is large or small, this strategy calls you to attend to those losses you feel, reminding you that ignoring them only increases the pain they ultimately bring into your life. It is important to remember you are not alone with your pain. This

strategy is designed to connect you to all of the women who have gone before you in working through a similar pregnancy loss. The strategy includes a simple process you can use to attend to your grief, and it ultimately will aid you in finding a place from which you can continue.

Each of these nine strategies increases your ability to move through the mental and emotional challenges of pregnancy as comfortably as possible. They give you the reassurance that your wild mix of intense feelings are one-hundred percent normal. They help you clarify what is uniquely best for you and then motivate you to take the necessary action to get what you need. These strategies give you a powerful place from which to operate and, when mixed in with the rest of your life, can allow your journey to be lighter, more interesting, richer with meaning and comfortably supported. So when the pregnancy is over and you hold that sweet little babe in your arms, welcoming your child into this life, you will have gracefully traversed your nine months of pregnancy, building your inner strength and peace of mind every step of the way.

Four Disciplines that Allow You to Make the Most of These Nine Strategies

There are four disciplines that, when followed, will give you the ability to take these nine strategies for peace of mind and personal power farther than you could ever imagine. There is nothing hip or trendy about adhering to these disciplines. Instead, it is a quiet commitment, an ongoing decision, a knowledge that in following a set of disciplines you will have more of what you want.

In working any disciplines, you are being asked to control your own behavior or train yourself to act in alignment with your chosen direction. The results you achieve from this effort may not be immediately obvious, but you can count on the fact that you are making slow, incremental changes towards your desired goal.

Committing to any discipline takes courage and perseverance. This is the courage to face your own truth and the perseverance to stay the course. A true discipline takes some effort to master and often presents itself as a circuitous pathway towards your ultimate destination. There is nothing particularly easy about any of these four disciplines, but, at the same time, they do not need to be hard. They are the kind of life tools that will aid you in anything you do. Take these disciplines to heart, let them keep you from limiting yourself, and use them to guide you in designing simplicity, comfort, balance and peace of mind into every part of your pregnancy.

THE FIRST DISCIPLINE: WATCH FOR YOUR OWN STUBBORN RESISTANCE

One of the most powerful human responses to change, challenge and newness in life is resistance. Pregnancy is an experience filled with all of this. You will know you are bumping into your own resistance when you find yourself:

➤ Going to ridiculous extremes to keep old and comfortable patterns or routines, even though they no longer fit.
➤ Dismissing an idea or concept even before you fully understand it.
➤ Labeling everything that is new as bad.
➤ Dragging your feet on something that you know in your head is important, but you just cannot seem to make your body do it.

When you see yourself showing some resistance, don't push it away and label yourself as wrong for feeling it. Instead move closer towards it and see what it is about. Why are you feeling this resistance? What don't you want to lose? What are you afraid of? What part feels too hard?

Then, once you understand where your resistance is coming from, look for ways to meet those concerns, wants or needs. Promise yourself that you do not have to lose what is important to you. Commit to looking for options until you are able to find one that you can live with. Then, if you have honestly done all this, the letting go should be easy. The resistance should shift and move away. You may find you still have some letting go to do, but this kind of letting go is about recognizing an ending or changing a habit. It's not about fighting with yourself or others.

THE SECOND DISCIPLINE: LOOK FOR YOUR HIDDEN OPPORTUNITIES

In everything you do there is the potential for opportunity. These opportunities are usually found by quieting useless chatter and listening to what ultimately matters most. By pausing and listening, you can gain the insight you need to put the evolving pieces of your pregnant life together in the way that best serves you in any situation.

Listening leads to increasing your self-awareness and, with self-awareness, you will uncover precious information about who you are and what you want. For example, by listening, you could find a new freedom to do something differently than you normally would, opening an invaluable array of options. This could be about letting go of perfectionism and giving yourself the freedom to just be you, perfect or not. It could be finding that you crave alone time and need to build blocks of unscheduled time into your life. Or maybe just the opposite is true and, you want the freedom to spend more time with the people you love. Whatever it is, the insight you gain from listening to yourself will be your own new-found treasure.

Begin by asking yourself several different questions and see where they take you. Some useful questions to consider are:

➤ What do I want?
➤ What do I need to let go of?
➤ What is next for me?
➤ What matters to me?
➤ What is most important in this situation?
➤ What support do I need?
➤ What do I need to do to take good care of myself in this situation?

For some people, it is helpful to write down their answers, others can just think about their answers and get all the assistance they need. There is no right or wrong answer. There is no good or bad answer. There is just your most thoughtful and fully conscious answer at this particular time.

THE THIRD DISCIPLINE: WATCH YOURSELF AND CATCH YOUR OWN EMOTIONAL BAD HABITS

This is like catching your own hand in the emotional cookie jar. But what is the bad habit in which you might be catching yourself?

It could be any number of bad habits that cause you to feel anything from annoyance to submissiveness, anger, frustration, disconnection or fear.

Whatever it is for you, the key is to catch them as early as possible and use them as guides to tell you what you need. If your bad habit is denial, maybe you need to stake a claim for something that is important to you. If your bad habit is self-pity, maybe you need to begin doing something that allows you to help yourself. If the habit is feeling overwhelmed, maybe you need to finally commit to letting go of enough so your life feels manageable. If the habit is giving too much, maybe you need to give yourself permission to do just want you want and not what other people want you to do.

Catching your own bad habits only works if you do it honestly. Taking time to catch the bad habits you think you should be catching, given what your mother or your father would have caught in a similar situation, is not honest. Catching just the "nice" bad habits inside of you is not honest. Catching just the bad habits you want to catch is not honest. Watching out for your own bad habits will only help you if you catch all that is there.

If you don't do this honestly and instead only try to deny that something exists, you will only increase its ability to get in your way. You may run the risk of ignoring some important information that is linked to your current situation. By going unconscious, you may be creating more work for yourself in the long run. These bad habits don't just go away.

Once you have caught a bad habit and see it for what it is, you can decide what you want or need to do with it. You can make choices about how to best handle whatever bad habit you have caught by taking actions such as:

> Noticing that a wave of your bad habit has just washed in and using your awareness of it as a great place to begin taking back control. Now you see what you might not have even considered before. In the wake of your habit, you can see it for what it is. This simple realization has you well on your way to kicking the habit. Then, the next time it starts rolling in your direction, you might catch it just a bit earlier than you did this time. When that happens, count it as a big win.

➤ Choosing to stop yourself whenever you see this bad habit appearing, in midsentence if you have to, and making a course correction.

➤ Going back to the situations or interactions where you now realize one of your bad habits had been running wild, and apologizing or otherwise setting things right.

➤ Taking some time to step back and reflect on the true impact of this bad habit on you, those around you and the larger community within which you live. Do this not to make yourself feel guilty but for the purpose of reminding yourself how much it does matter that you make a change.

➤ Asking someone close to you to let you know when he or she sees you falling into the bad habit you are trying to break.

In the end, you are looking for an action that will break the grip this habit has over you and give you some room to make decisions and interact with others from outside its limiting structure.

Your job in catching these is not to expect perfection right away. Your job is to be aware. In this discipline, you are raising your awareness and moving forward one baby step at a time. There is no room for beating yourself up for doing something wrong. That will only get you caught in another bad habit called self-punishment. While you are pregnant, your focus should be on taking care of yourself and this little baby growing inside of you. There will be no better time than now to begin this process of honest self-noticing. You have a great excuse. People expect you to want and need more right now. Begin doing what is truly important.

The Fourth Discipline: Good or Bad, Experience Whatever Your Pregnancy Brings

The last discipline is short and sweet but equally powerful. Whatever your pregnancy brings to you, good or bad, challenging or exhilarating, keep yourself open to experience it all. Don't let yourself gloss over the good or shut out the bad; each is a part of living, and each has something to offer. If you do choose not to address something now, at least make this a very conscious choice and know that, by ignoring it, you will likely be missing out on some of the living along the way.

By trying to numb out the parts of the pregnancy experience you don't like, you will inevitably be cutting off your opportunity to enjoy some of the other parts. Without the help of an anesthesiologist, it is virtually impossible to numb one part of you and not include many other parts as well. To take part in all the richness pregnancy brings, you must be alive for all of it. To some, this may sound intimidating at first. But if you keep your courage and begin living this way, you will soon find the peace of mind it offers. By allowing yourself to openly feel the painful times, you will actually be able to move more quickly through the hard emotions and find yourself feeling the comforts of pleasant times that much sooner.

Your Place of Brilliance

Within each of us there is place of brilliance. This is the place where the true you comes to life. Here you are able to shine out above anything that is happening around you. It is the best that you have to bring to yourself, your baby and the world.

In addition to increasing your peace of mind during pregnancy, these four disciplines and nine strategies will bring you closer to your own brilliance. They are simple tools that will help you powerfully push aside any blocks that may be limiting the luster of all you have to bring. They are a safe and comfortable refuge when the challenges of pregnancy leave you feeling like that strong and brilliant place is too hard to find. They are a stabilizing force that can keep you clear about what matters most when so much remains unclear. They are one way to allow yourself to create the conditions whereby you are able to be the best you can, in all of the experiences of your pregnancy and beyond.

Use each strategy as it is needed throughout your pregnancy. Find the gift, the life lesson, that each of the nine strategies has to offer to you, during and after your pregnancy. Pass this gift along to that beautiful little baby growing inside of you, as well as to the next pregnant woman you find in need of a helping hand.

RESOURCES

On Pregnancy

Your Pregnancy Week by Week, Glade B. Curtis and Judith Schuler. (Fisher Books, 2000.)

The Unofficial Guide to Having a Baby, Ann Douglas and John R. Sussman MD. (Hungry Minds, Inc., 1999.)

While Waiting, George E. Verrilli, Anne Marie Mueser and Marie Mueser. (Griffin Trade Paperback, 1998, 2nd revised edition.)

Mama's Little Baby: The Black Woman's Guide to Pregnancy, Childbirth, and Baby's First Year, Dennis Brown, Pamela Toussaint and Mona Mark. (New York, NY: Dutton, 1997.)

The Pregnancy Book: Month-by-Month, Everything You Need to Know From America's Baby Experts, William Sears, Martha Sears and Linda H. Holt. (New York, NY: Little Brown and Company, 1997.)

The Pregnancy Journal; A Day-To-Day Guide to a Healthy and Happy Pregnancy, A. Christine Harris, Ph.D. (San Francisco, CA: Chronicle Books, 1996.)

The Blue Jay's Dance: A Birth Year, Louise Erdrich. (New York, NY: Harper Perennial, 1995.)

The Girlfriends' Guide to Pregnancy: Or Everything Your Doctor Won't Tell You, Vicki Iovine. (New York, NY: Pocket Books, 1995.)

An Easier Childbirth: A Mother's Workbook for Health and Emotional Well-Being During Pregnancy and Delivery, Gayle Peterson, Ph.D. (Los Angeles, CA: JP Tarcher, 1991.)

A Child Is Born: Dramatic Photographs of Life Before Birth, Lennart Nilsson. (New York, NY: Dell Trade Publications, 1986.)

Baby Center, www.babycenter.com
General information on pregnancy and caring for you baby.

BirthPlan.com, www.birthplan.com
An interactive birth plan maker.

Childbirth.org, www.childbirth.org
A site dedicated to providing information and resources to pregnant women and their partners so they can make the best choices for themselves. Once at the site, search under the topic in which you are interested.

Fit Pregnancy, www.fitpregnancy.com
A magazine and online website focused on issues of pregnancy and beyond.

The Labor of Love, www.thelaboroflove.com
A pregnancy and parenting support center.

Pregnancy Today, www.pregnancytoday.com
The online journal for parents to be.

STRATEGY ONE

GIVE YOURSELF THE BEST BY CREATING AND CALLING UPON A COMMITTED SUPPORT SYSTEM

You are very capable, and, yes it's true, you have the ability to do all of this pregnancy stuff without a shred of support. However, pregnancy is not some kind of endurance test, and the point is not about whether you can do it all on your own but how you can take the best care of yourself throughout the whole process. Pregnancy alone can be a long, isolating road. Life is so complex, and the birth experience has the potential to be so rich, why would you want anything less than the best for both you and your unborn baby?

Choosing to go through pregnancy with a supportive community creates a wealth of resources from which you can draw. This community can include an intimately involved pregnancy partner, as well as those who are less involved but providing other kinds of support. The involvement and companionship of others gives you people to call upon for information, emotional support, domestic assistance, celebration and grieving.

The focus of this kind of a supportive community is you. Your pregnancy is a time for receiving. This kind of support can be tough for a lot of people to accept. So if it will help at all, keep in mind that, in ways you may not even realize, by receiving this support, you are giving back. You are:

> Sharing this grand journey that can improve family and community ties by uniting many through the anticipation

and fresh sense of hope that comes with the birth of a child.

➤ Reminding people of the miracle of birth which gives those
involved an opportunity for a new beginning in their lives
and brings the possibility for renewal to even the most
casual of acquaintances.

➤ Providing an opportunity for those who care about you to
physically demonstrate this care, allowing them to feel their
importance in your life.

So open yourself up to all of the support that is out there
for you.

Creating a Pregnancy Partnership

A cornerstone of building pregnancy support is to find a
committed partner. This is a person whom you have welcomed into
every aspect of your pregnancy and who is with you as a pillar of
support to walk throughout the entire nine months at your side. A
caring and committed partner can provide peace of mind and

assistance through the twists
and turns of pregnant life.
Pregnant women can give
back to their partners by
providing them with the
opportunity to be an active
participant in the creation
of a new life. Kristen found
her way into just such
a relationship.

*When I was pregnant
with my first baby, I
unconsciously stumbled into
a wonderful pregnancy
partnership. Early on, my
husband just sort of meta-*
*morphosed into my pregnancy partner. And as we moved through
the nine months together, I began to realize how powerful it was to
have a close partner in this process. I was so thankful he was by my
side. He didn't come to this role of pregnancy partner with any*

special expertise or experience. He was as blind as I was about pregnancy and childbirth, maybe even more so. But I got all I needed from my partnership with him. He was in no way perfect and, as could be expected, we definitely irritated each other along the way. But he gave me great support and care. I had an active and interested partner in this process, as well as someone I loved to share the emotional intimacy I value and craved during my pregnancy.

The following sections give you some things to consider as you create your unique version of a pregnancy partnership with someone you trust.

FINDING YOUR PARTNER

For many of you, like Kristen, choosing this person is a no-brainer. You're married to him or she is your life partner, this person is your most intimate connection and deepest bond to another human being. Of course, he's the one; of course, she'll be there for you. For others, the actual act of choosing a partner may be less cut and dried. You may be having a baby as a single woman or you may be committed to a person upon whom you cannot rely as your principle partner through the pregnancy. Perhaps he's overwhelmed in another area of his life, or she is traveling much of the time. Maybe he doesn't have the ability to be supportive of you at this time, or she just doesn't seem to understand about the pregnancy. For those of you who do not have a pregnancy partner built into your life partner, you will need to look to other areas of your life. So, where can you find a supportive pregnancy partner who will be able to commit to you and your pregnancy process? You could look to a:

> Father
> Mother
> Cousin
> Sister-in-law
> Friend
> Grandparent
> Aunt
> Doula (See resource section for further information.)
> Co-worker

There is no right or wrong partner as long as you feel good about working with him or her. He or she must be willing to commit to the pregnancy process with you.

How do you choose the best pregnancy partner? The best way to make a solid decision is to raise your self-awareness about whom you are truly comfortable with and explore the possibilities with brutal honesty. This is the kind of honesty that gives you the freedom to step away from "shoulds," familiar traps or the "right things" so you can consider what is important to you. Listening to this honesty inside of you means you are picking your principle support person based on what feels best to you rather than on what others may want you to do. Begin by considering your own personal style, perspectives and what you want from a pregnancy  partner. Here are some questions you could ask yourself to gain insight in these areas:

- ➤ Who can support me through my biggest fears?
- ➤ What will I need the most from my pregnancy partner?
- ➤ What person in my life has been very reliable or come through for me in the past?
- ➤ Whom can I be with at my worst moments and feel like it's okay?
- ➤ Who would be good at helping me transition through all of the changes this pregnancy will bring?
- ➤ What kind of commitment do I want?
- ➤ With whom would I feel comfortable in very physically or emotionally intimate situations? Consider this person from three perspectives: before the intimate situation happens, during the situation and after the situation has occurred.
- ➤ Who is able to manage well under pressure?

➤ Whom do I know that is reassuring and has a calming or soothing effect on me?

Some logistical considerations might be:

➤ Where would I want my partner to be physically located?

➤ How flexible will I need him to be?

➤ With how many different kinds of things will I want her to help?

➤ What strengths or abilities would I like my partener to have?

➤ What kind of childbirth experience do I want her to have?

➤ How do I feel about the impact of his own life and commitments on this partnership?

As you decide upon your preferred partner, the point is not to hold out for perfection. Instead listen to what you notice inside of you and see who seems to stand out from the others in your life.

DESIGNING YOUR NEW PARTNERSHIP TOGETHER

Whether a spouse or another person you trust, start by talking together about what you want from this partnership. A helpful place to begin is to agree this partnership will be built on a foundation of three very simple but powerful tenants:

➤ Mutual respect

➤ A commitment to stay the course

➤ Plenty of room to talk openly

These three tenants will give you the foundation needed to maneuver through anything a pregnancy can throw your way. Some other quetions to consider discussing with your partner include:

➤ What is his interest in the pregnancy process?

➤ Why is it important to have her involved?

➤ Which aspects are of primary importance which are secondary?

➤ What does he not want to be part of?

➤ How will her initial role in the process be defined? (This may shift with some of the pregnancy-related changes you face.)

➤ What kind of time commitment is he willing to make in both normal times and if something like bedrest becomes necessary in the pregnancy?

➤ What are your ideas about working together through labor and delivery?

➤ What excites each of you most about the pregnancy?

➤ What special requests do you have of one another?

➤ How will the two of you begin working together?

➤ How will you communicate with each other? For example, will you set up a regular meal together, call one another on a regular basis or be there for each other whenever needed to get a handle on a stressful pregnancy-related experience?

The basic goal of these questions is to assist each of you in clarifying what it means to work together in a partnership through the birth of this baby.

SETTING UP YOUR PREGNANCY PARTNER FOR SUCCESS

Yes, you are the one having the baby, but to be a good resource to you, your pregnancy partner needs to get some care as well. Both of you may be experiencing your first birth of a baby. Neither of you may be sure about what to do, so it is important you look out for one another and help each other along the way.

One of the best things you can do to take good care of your pregnancy partner is to talk with her about what is going on with you and the pregnancy. If your partner is going to be fully involved, you need to include her. Tell her how it feels to be struggling with a current concern, ask her to do some reading on a procedure you are going to receive, get her insight into a particular issue and don't forget to include her in the diversity of joys through the process.

You can take care of your pregnancy partner by assisting him with the challenges he is facing about the birth of this child. If he is going to be a new parent, he will also be going through a lot of his own emotions, as he finds his way into parenthood. He may be:

➤ Unsure of his future role as a parent.

➤ Nervous about how pregnancy and the baby will change your life together.

➤ Concerned about the finances related to pregnancy and raising children.

Whether your partner will be a parent to your child or not, all pregnancy partners could be:

➤ Struggling with some of the same challenges you are going through.

➤ Feeling insecure about her level of knowledge on the topic of pregnancy and childbirth.

➤ Anxious about what your pregnancy will demand of her.

➤ Uncomfortable with the changes that have resulted in your lifestyle.

➤ Unsure of being a good partner for you.

➤ Uncomfortable with medical situations.

➤ Nervous about what she has become committed to.

➤ Sad about the coming changes in your relationship with one another.

Being able to return support to this person throughout the nine months will allow your partner to be even more helpful and reliable to you when you need him. It can also have a wonderfully positive impact on your shifting relationship.

Today, unlike twenty-five years ago, there are many husbands, life partners and committed friends interested in and able to be involved in the entire pregnancy process with the women they love. The medical world is slowly responding to this by attempting to make room for partners' participation. Partners take an active role in the hospitals' birthing classes, and their presence is often assumed through labor and delivery. But many practitioners do little to include partners in the routine ins and outs of the process. Partners are often left on the sidelines and unsure about what to do or say. However, that is not how it has to be. The two of you get to determine together how you want to navigate all of this and with a little bit of dancing around hospital- or doctor-mandated policies, you can have it the way you want it. Here is how that dance went for Alicia and her partner Kenny:

My pregnancy partner is my husband, and he wants to be involved in this process from the beginning to the end. He has come to almost all of my midwife visits, and I love that he wants to be such a big part of the pregnancy. At the same time, I think it can be a challenging role. There is no clear path telling him how to be supportive, and I don't know how to make it easier for him. I basically have no idea what I am doing myself. Our midwives don't say much about the role of the pregnancy partner. They seem to do their job with me, the patient, and just make the room for us to do whatever we want to do together. I can understand this orientation. I'm sure every woman and her pregnancy partner want something a little different. The challenge for us as first-time parents is we have no guidance in how to do this together, and we don't necessarily know what we need or even want.

This awkwardness showed up at our most recent midwife visit. We were just to the point of hearing the baby's heartbeat. This is a special time for me right now; it is my only tangible evidence of this baby's existence. So at this climactic moment of the entire visit, my husband says, "We forgot to tie the dog up when we left the car." Great, I thought, here we are, hearing the positive sign of life in our unborn child, and you are over there talking about the dog. I tried to ignore him.

When we walked out, I asked that he keep those kinds of random thoughts to himself when we are listening to the baby's heartbeat or, for that matter, any time I am on the examining table with the midwife. He felt bad. As we continued to talk, what became clear to both of us was that he did not feel very important in this process. He felt uncomfortable and unclear about his role in the examining room with me. He didn't know where to stand or what to do with himself. In his discomfort, he said less-than-appropriate things at less-than-appropriate times.

In the distraction of his awkwardness, he also missed this wondrous event. He did not pay attention to the beating heart of this new life, and he missed important information the midwife gave us. He was too distracted by thoughts of where to look and how he should be.

I can empathize with his discomfort. Here he is at his wife's medical appointment. She's naked under an office wrap and sitting up on a table with all kinds of bizarre things going on. Plus, let's face it — I am the main event here. It is all about the baby, my body and me. The medical folks are not overly interested in my husband. They are nice to him, and they answer his questions, but they aren't going out of their way to make him feel special or needed.

We began talking about his role. We identified where he should stand when I am on the examining table. We discussed the ways that he is important for us and our baby during our pregnancy. And we talked about the fact that involved dads are still somewhat rare in this process and that we may need to do some educating of our healthcare practitioners regarding his role. This is our baby, and I want us sharing all the joys and pains of this child from the very beginning.

How do you want to have your pregnancy partner involved in the medically oriented portions of your pregnancy? What will be comfortable for you and your partner? What will ensure you get the support you want?

Your pregnancy partner is a unique individual, and you cannot truly know what he or she wants until you ask. Take the time to talk about what would be the most helpful — and then listen carefully to what you are told.

Now go get your partner; this next section is one you will want to read together.

FIVE ACTIONS PARTNERS CAN TAKE TO KNOCK THE SOCKS OFF THE PREGNANT WOMAN IN THEIR LIVES

Hello, partners. Much of this book has information you will find helpful, but this section in particular speaks directly to you.

You have signed on as a pregnancy partner, you may have talked a bit with the pregnant woman in your life about what that means, but still, what are you supposed to do? Here are five very tangible and simple things you can do throughout the pregnancy, which will allow you to be an amazing pregnancy partner to this woman you love.

First: Take the Time to Slow Down and Listen to Her. Hear what she has to say, listen to her concerns and try to understand them. Listen to what matters to her and share in her excitement. This sounds like no big deal, you do it all the time, right? Maybe not — most people are so busy doing so many things, it is hard for them to stop and listen. Many people will get as far as stopping their activities in order to pay attention, but their minds are still racing in ten different directions. They may be catching every other word, just enough to produce an intelligent response, but they are not listening. Sitting and listening is one of the biggest gifts you can give someone, especially a pregnant woman.

Second: Accompany Her to Prenatal Appointments. Most women can clearly handle this on their own; they don't need you to be there. However, it is a great time for connecting with each other around the baby. It keeps you linked into the process. It helps you begin to understand the baby's development and keeps you connected with all of the gradual changes in your pregnant partner's body. The two of you get to hear the heartbeat together, take that scary test together or get some new information about your baby together. The value in sharing this experience is that it belongs to both of you; it's not just another experience about which she tells you.

Third: Help Her with All of the Ordinary and Mundane Tasks of Life. These are things like meals, shopping, household chores, preparing for the baby or caring for older children. Again, for some women, getting all of this "normal life" stuff done becomes a big deal, and others hardly even skip a beat — they add all of the new-baby activities and preparations into their life and happily continue storming through the day, accomplishing all they need to. The key is to talk about how you can be helpful. While these mundane tasks may seem obvious, it can be hard to know where help is needed when a pregnancy is presenting such a rapid progression of changes and challenges.

Fourth: Give of Yourself in Small, Simple Ways. Bring her a flower from your garden, give her a little back rub, light a special candle or bring her favorite food. Make an effort to give some of your time to learning more about pregnancy, childbirth and babies. Now you're not just an interested participant, you are a valuable resource for her. If you are going to be a parent to this child, maybe you give her the gift of doing things to proactively build your bond with your unborn child. You could do this by talking to the baby through your partner's tummy, taking the time to pick a special gift for the child or initiating a conversation about how the two of you want to parent together. You could give her the gift of attentiveness. To do this, check in with her at social situations to see how she is doing. Sit down next to her and ask her what she is thinking about. Set up a mystery outing to surprise her. The list of inexpensive, yet meaningful, gifts you can give is only limited by the bounds of your imagination.

Fifth: Pay Attention to What the Pregnant Woman in Your Life Says She Wants. If you are ever in doubt of what is helpful, just ask her. If you are ever unsure of what to be doing, check it out. Some specific things that pregnant women often wish their partners would do include:

➤ Taking time out to focus more on her, your pregnant partner. All of the attention can get focused on the baby inside or the demands of your life, and often pregnant women would appreciate it if you could take a couple of moments and pay attention to them. Some fun suggestions are to create a special audiotape or compact disc of music for her pregnancy, spontaneously offer to take her out for her favorite treat or hide a small surprise in her home or car.

➤ Making time to do more baby-related research. She might like it if you would look through the name books, read up on the next phase of pregnancy or begin researching how to care for your new baby.

You were chosen to be this woman's pregnancy partner because she loves and trusts you. She wants to share this miraculous time with you. Pause to notice the simple, beautiful pleasures that go along with the whole process; it will benefit you as much as your partner. Then commit yourself to make a beautiful partnership with this woman you care about.

FINDING YOUR WAY INTO PARTNERSHIP TOGETHER

In this partnership, the two of you have the opportunity to

create something you want both for yourselves and the new baby you are bringing into the world. Whatever your previous commitments to one another have been, you have just begun a new or additional nine-month commitment, unlike most anything you have experienced before.

And, yes, you can expect to hit some major bumps along the way. Even if you are both committed and excited, even if you're both very good at listening and treat one another with all of the respect you both deserve, you will still disagree at times. You will still bug each other sometimes. You will still piss off each other. This is real life. Unfortunately, even when you are a glowing vessel of life, you don't get to live in "happily ever after" land.

Facing pregnancy together includes having breakdowns with each other and then picking yourselves up and putting all of the pieces back together to take your next step forward. It is about looking at what you can create together, keeping that image as the centerpiece to guide your actions and decisions. It is about supporting one another. It is about asking each other the tough questions. It is about just being there with each other.

Through it all, remember the two of you are not alone. Reach out to your larger community often to gain additional insight, information, guidance or support. Recognize the strength available to you from inside yourself and within your partner. Give yourselves room to struggle when you need to. You will be able to navigate all that is to come if you laugh easily and often, acknowledge the challenges in the situations you face, cherish the joys and take each moment as it comes.

Building a Whole Community of Support

A pregnancy partner is essential to great support, but one person cannot provide you with all of the support you need. A community is able to pick up where your partner leaves off. A supportive community surrounds you with many different dimensions of support.

➤ Your life partner who brings love and commitment
➤ A friend who brings womanly connection and camaraderie
➤ A doula who brings professional expertise

➢ A midwife or doctor who brings life-saving knowledge
➢ A parent who can remember your time in the womb
➢ A special neighbor who is so close and convenient
➢ A member of your religious organization with whom you enjoy spending time
➢ A co-worker with whom you share something in common

What a group to have supporting you through your pregnancy! With that kind of support, the ups and downs of your pregnancy could almost be as comfortable as your familiar hammock gently swaying in a warm summer breeze.

Building this kind of a supportive community is not a one-shot deal; it is an ongoing process. You must intentionally and actively reach out to those around you, engaging them in conversation, showing an interest in their lives and welcoming them into yours. You cannot expect a neighbor to be a comforting part of your support community when you hardly ever see each other. This kind of a community takes some effort on your part, but it gives back much more than it takes.

DECIDING WHAT YOU WANT FROM YOUR COMMUNITY

The first thing you need to do is figure out what kind of support you want. At first glance, you may say, a partner, friend, doula, midwife, what more could a pregnant woman want? But there are also many other interesting ways you can feel supported during this time. Here are some things to consider as you begin to decide what you want from your comforting community of support.

➢ Telephone assistance from your healthcare provider, who responds with support and patience to even your most paranoid of fears
➢ A midwife or doctor who takes the time needed to answer all of your questions and adds insightful comments that help you along in the process
➢ A person in your life who will pause amid the business of his life to take pictures throughout your pregnancy, capturing the miracle of your changing body
➢ A friend who has already been pregnant and invites you to call anytime in any physical or emotional state to talk

about your latest pregnancy woe
- ➤ A neighbor, co-worker or friend with older children who has been through all of this before
- ➤ A gathering of pregnant women with whom you can share your experiences

The possibilities are endless, and all of these people add another layer to the support you know you have to call upon.

With a clearer idea of what you want, ask yourself whom you want to give you this support? Where can you find these people in your life? Do you need to look at switching your healthcare providers? Finding other pregnant women? Reconnecting with a distant relative?

It is also important to realize that the support you need may evolve throughout your pregnancy. As your body changes and your baby grows, your need for physical support may increase. As you get closer and closer to labor, you may want more mental and emotional support to help you through your final weeks and the grand conclusion of labor. As you begin to parent your baby, you may find you want supportive guidance from someone who has experience with babies, or you may need the pinnacle of support at this stage in the game, a two-hour break so you can get some sleep. Stacy saw this evolution very dramatically at critical points in her second pregnancy.

When I was pregnant with our second child, my husband and I both started out on the same track. We were both very distracted with our young son and our work and the thought of getting everything done before our second baby came. Then my focus began to shift towards our new baby and taking time to simply enjoy this pregnancy.

My husband did not make this transition with me. He stayed distracted and focused on all the outside issues. I began to feel alone with the pregnancy. I felt sad for this baby, and I didn't feel like my husband and I were making a very good team. I began to worry about labor and how we would do that together since we were on such different tracks.

We spoke about my concerns a lot, but it didn't seem to make a difference in my feelings. We loved having just the two of us and the hospital staff at the first birth, and that was our plan with this baby. But I was beginning to feel worried that, given his orientation and mine, it would not be enough.

Then I realized that in looking for support from my husband I was comparing everything about this pregnancy to the first one — trying to have the same wonderful experience a second time around. This wasn't helping me, my husband or our new, unborn child. I realized I needed some support other than my husband. I needed to find someone who could just be excited with me about the coming of this baby. I also needed to let my expectations go and just let it be what it was — its own new, unique experience.

The bottom line is pay attention to what you want and need from your community of support. Ask for new things when you see a change in your needs. The original community may not be able to meet every need, but they can't even try if you don't at least ask.

Strike a Healthy Balance When Seeking Support

As with most things in life, there is a natural balance to getting support. Too much and you drown, too little and you're left cold and alone, shivering on the edge of the pool. You know you're striking a nice balance for yourself when you feel some of the following:

> ➤ You have someone to turn to for almost all situations that arise.
> ➤ You feel well-informed.
> ➤ You are confident that you will find a way to handle whatever surprises this pregnancy brings.
> ➤ You have lots of good information, as well as the room to make your own decisions.

You know you are not in balance if you spot these symptoms too often in your days or nights:

> ➤ You feel frozen or unable to act without the explicit advice of one or more people.
> ➤ You feel isolated, alone or cut off a significant amount of the time.
> ➤ You feel uninformed.
> ➤ You notice those who are supporting you begin to respond negatively to your requests.

➤ You feel overwhelmed by information.

Experiencing each of these unsupported feelings at points in your pregnancy is a normal part of the process. It begins to become a warning sign of unbalanced support when you feel it consistently over a period of time or when you become uncomfortable with how often it is happening. Let's look at what you can do to maintain or get yourself back in step with your own natural balance.

1. Learn the best ways you can support yourself. What are the actions you can take that leave you feeling supported? These could be:

➤ Allowing yourself to call your clinic's nurse line without any hesitation.

➤ Having some good friends you can and will call when you feel low.

➤ Picking up a collection of books that have something important to say to you.

➤ Setting aside your fear of asking for help.

2. Get clear on what kind of support is helpful and what kind is not. The last thing you need is to catch someone else's angst or anxiety in the name of gaining support for yourself. Put some distance between yourself and those things or people that seem to make your situation worse instead of better. This might mean:

➤ Avoiding the topic of pregnancy with friends who continually tell you "horror" stories.

➤ Switching your medical care if you feel your current provider is adding to your worries rather than calming them.

➤ Putting away a resource that is causing you distress.

3. Learn what your warning signs are so you know when your support is out of whack in either direction. It is hard to do much of anything to make a course correction if you are unaware of any problem. For those of you who sit alone with a problem and never ask for any help or guidance, watch for warning signs such as needing information, feeling alone or experiencing an internal resistance to asking for help. Then burst out of your routine and ask for some help.

On the flip side, for those of you who fall into the trap of supportaholism, you will also want to uncover the markers along the way that clue you in to the fact you are going overboard. Watch out for exhaustion from information overload, confusion from the divergent advice you have received or the realization that you now have five more worries than you had when you began your quest for support. Pay close attention to reactions when you make requests. You may want to check in with a support person and see if you are asking for too much. If you know drowning in too much support can be your tendency, you could set some limits for yourself up front, such as:

> Only calling three friends on each new issue you face.

> Only reading about the situation you are facing in two books.

> Limiting the amount of time you will gather data from the web.

> Only making one request a day, week or month from any one person providing you with support.

> Checking in with those supporting you to see if you have been making too many requests.

A good balance should give you a comforting peace of mind and keep you, and those supporting you, from feeling overwhelmed. In finding your balance, you can trust you will get the support you need without either side feeling overwhelmed.

TEST YOUR WILLINGNESS TO RECEIVE SUPPORT

Below is an assessment to help you uncover how willing you are to allow yourself to be supported by others. You can surround yourself with the comfort of helping hands, but if you are not willing to reach out and grab one, all of these supportive hands will be of no help. Now that you are pregnant, test out the strength of your grip by reading each of the questions below and circling the answer that best fits you. If you cannot choose between two of the possible answers, circle them both.

1. I usually ask for help from someone who does not live with me:
   a. Once a week.
   b. Once a month.
   c. I cannot remember the last time.

2. The thing that usually keeps me from asking for help is that:
   a. I forget to ask.
   b. I feel like it is too much of a burden to ask.

    c. I feel like I am a weak person if I cannot do it all myself.

    d. All of the above.

3. I usually ask for help or support from the people I live with:

    a. Once an hour.

    b. Once a day.

    c. Once a week.

    d. I cannot remember the last time I asked for help.

4. When I think about the kind of support or help I'd like from others:

    a. I am very clear about what I want.

    b. I have some ideas about what would be helpful.

    c. I have no idea what kind of support or help to ask for.

5. When it comes to support and getting help, I basically operate on the principle of:

    a. Ask for what I need from the person best able to help me.

    b. If I need help, someone will show up to help me.

    c. I can handle it all and don't need to ask for help from anybody.

6. When asking for help, I:

    a. Continue asking until I get what I need.

    b. Only ask those few people I know don't mind helping me.

    c. Ask once and, if they say no, I give up.

7. The way I usually ask for help or support is to:

    a. Call one of my friends or family and make a request.

    b. Wait for someone to offer something and then ask for what I need.

    c. Look needy and hope someone notices I need help or support.

8. If I need some help or support about an emotional issue:

    a. I call a person right when I need that support and work through it, emotions and all.

    b. I wait until all of the emotion is gone and then call and tell my supportive friend what I have been going through.

    c. I don't call anyone and only talk about it with a friend if the topic happens to come up.

9. When I need support:
    a. I know exactly whom to call for what.
    b. I am unsure about whom to call, but I usually stumble across someone who can help.
    c. I feel very alone and have no idea who can help me.

10. When it comes to having enough pregnancy information I feel:
    a. I have all the information I need.
    b. I wish I had more.
    c. I feel like I am missing out on information that could make this whole experience much easier.

When you have circled at least one response to each of the questions, compute your score by giving yourself:

➤ 1 point for every "a" circled.
➤ 2 points for every "b" circled.
➤ 3 points for every "c" circled.
➤ 4 points for every "d" circled.
➤ And on those questions where you could not decide between two answers, take the average of the two numbers. For example, if you circled both answer "a" and "b" for one of the questions because you saw yourself doing both, give yourself 1.5 for that question, the average of the two answers. Now tally up your score.

If your score is between 10 and 19.5

Congratulations! You're doing well asking for, and likely getting, the support you need. If you face a challenge about seeking pregnancy support, it leans towards seeking too much rather than too little. You may want to reread the last paragraph of the previous section, "Striking A Healthy Balance When Seeking Support," and pay close attention to see if anything rings true in your life.

If your score is between 20 and 29.5

It is time to turn it up a bit. During pregnancy and again in early parenthood, the support of others is vital. So read through your responses and pick one question where you would like to make improvements. Pick a question where you could aim for the "a" response.

If your score is between 30 and 40

It is time to make building a support system one of your top priorities. Even if you happen to be one of the lucky few who have a dream pregnancy, you still need some form of support just to process all of the personal transitions coming your way. Your homework is to review the questions above, pick three areas that would dramatically increase the support in your life, and then identify several specific actions you can take right now to incorporate that support. Commit to doing something every week to strengthen the support you are getting during your pregnancy. If you are stuck for things to do, flip through the other eight strategies in the book. On these pages, you will find hundreds of suggestions you can take to increase the level of help or support in your life.

FINDING THE COURAGE TO ASK FOR SOME SUPPORT

Now comes the big challenge for a lot of people, the actual asking. Knowing what you want is an essential beginning, but it will get you nowhere unless you are willing to ask. Your final step to a community of great support is to take responsibility for getting the assistance you want. Don't sit back and wait for it to just arrive at your door because, even with the most caring of friends, it probably won't happen that way. And even if it did, it likely would not be the kind of support you needed at the time anyway. The bottom line is you are the one who is ultimately responsible for making sure you have the support you need. Here are some ways you could begin asking.

> ➤ If asking for support is extremely hard for you, as it is for many people, think ahead about what others could do for you. Then when someone offers something you want, take him or her up on it right then and there.

> ➤ Contact those people included in your ideal support system through this pregnancy and ask them if they would be willing to help you out during this time. Be sure to tell them specifically what you would like from them. Chances are they will

be honored to be someone you want involved during your pregnancy, so use the support they have offered you.

➤ Make a commitment to yourself that you will seek out some support or help at least once per week. No matter what, make yourself get some support. In the long run, you will feel much better for it, and you will likely find it easier to ask for help as time goes by.

➤ Place a big support reminder in your house, someplace you often go to when life is extra challenging. One of the biggest barriers to getting the support is that getting through a tough situation can be so consuming that you forget to ask. So, strategically place that reminder while the going is good. Then you will have the support you need when it gets a lot harder.

As a final note, in addition to making use of your great support system, it is also important you take some time to appreciate the gifts these people are giving you. These gifts are far better than any material items. Their result is the peace of mind that can only be found in the support of others and the accompanying realization that you are not alone. You can't put a price on the value of this kind of mental peace and personal serenity.

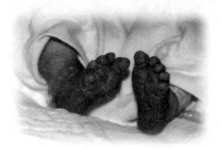

Summary

Don't Wait Until You are on the Brink of Collapse to Get Some Support!

The Calming Peace of Mind That Comes From This Kind of Support
- ➤ You know that no matter what happens, you have the support you want.
- ➤ You have a safe place to process some of your most intense feelings about the pregnancy.
- ➤ You will receive help from others without feeling that you are taking advantage of them.
- ➤ You develop a connection in a special, new way with some important family members or friends.
- ➤ You know it is okay for you to ask for what you want in terms of support from those around you.

What It Will Require to Be Your Own Best Supporter
- ➤ You must set your relentless pride and self-sufficiency aside and find the courage to ask for the help you need or want.
- ➤ You need to open yourself up with other people, letting them see who you are behind the public face they usually see.
- ➤ You must learn to listen to what your head, heart and intuition are telling you about how you want to be supported.
- ➤ It is time to let go of any "shoulds" and do what you need to do to take good care of yourself.

Resources

On Pregnancy Partnerships and Labor Support

The Birth Partner, Second Edition, Penny Simkin. (Boston, MA: Harvard Common Press, 2001.)

Special Women: The Role of the Professional Labor Assistant, Paulina Perez and Cheryl Snedeker. (Cutting Edge Press, 1994.)

Mothering the Mother: How a Doula Can Help You Have a Shorter, Easier and Healthier Birth, Marshall H. Klaus, Phyllis H. Klaus and John Kennell. (Perseus Press, 1993.)

American Academy of Husband-Coached Childbirth, www.bradleybirth.com
This organization offers a specific method of partner-coached labor and childbirth training called The Bradley Method of Natural Childbirth.
Phone: (800) 422-4784
Address: Box 5224, Sherman Oaks, CA 91413-5224

DONA (Doulas of North America), www.dona.com
A doula is a trained professional who assists pregnant women through the process of labor and delivery. Contact this organization to find a doula in your area.
Phone: (801) 756-7331
Address: 13513 North Grove Drive, Alpine, UT 84004

Lamaze International, www.lamaze.org
A nonprofit association dedicated to promoting normal, natural, healthy and fulfilling childbearing experiences for women and their families through education, advocacy and reform.
Phone: (800) 368-4404
Address: Administrative Office, 2025 M Street, Suite 800, Washington, DC 20036-3309

On Building Community

Wisdom Circles: A Guide to Self-Discovery and Community Building in Small Groups, Charles Garfield, Cindy Spring and Sedonia Cahill. (New York, NY: Hyperion, 1999.)

On Listening

Listen Up: How to Improve Relationships, Reduce Stress and Be More Productive by Using the Power of Listening, Larry Lee Barker, Ph.D. and Kittie W. Watson, Ph. D. (New York, NY: St. Martin's Press, 2000.)

The Zen of Listening: Mindful Communication In The Age of Distraction, Rebecca Z. Shafir. (Quest Books, 2000.)

Strategy Two

Allow Yourself to Let Go of Social Standards and Create a New Relationship with Your Body

You likely went into your pregnancy expecting immense physical change and, depending on what kind of pregnancy you're having and how far along you are, you are probably experiencing much of what you anticipated. But are you also noticing these changes are impacting you far beyond the scope of your physical body? Are you finding that your sense of who you understand yourself to be is changing in ways you did not expect? Are you bumping into some challenges about what your body is becoming? Are you aware of some new expectations you didn't even know you had for yourself? Are these physical changes and all of the resulting implications gnawing away at your overall peace of mind?

The personal change that often accompanies pregnancy's physical change is usually unexpected, and it can catch you off guard. In pregnancy, the functioning of the body is taking center stage and, at the same time, the effects of these changes on all of the nonphysical parts of you deserve a little attention.

Let's give these physically induced mental and emotional challenges some time in the spotlight by first doing a little commiserating about all of the mixed up feelings your changing body can bring. Then, we can move on to present you with key tools and new perspectives for increasing your comfort with the dramatic and beautiful metamorphosis of your body. Finally, we will spend some time supporting those of you whose bodies are requiring you to live with more significant physical limitations, providing you with the ability to successfully accept and then navigate through the restrictions of your current reality.

Commiserating Over Mixed Feelings

You are pregnant and your body is creating a beautiful baby. The physical reality of this is that your stomach is sticking out in one direction, your butt is stretching out in the opposite direction and it can feel like you are turning into a walking bookshelf. Your growing body is miraculous and at the same time a gigantic confusion in your life. Physically, there is so much changing inside of you, who wouldn't have a host of mixed feelings? No matter who you are or what values you hold, bodies are important, and it can be uncomfortable when they respond or look different than you may be used to, even if it is for the sake of the baby. Let's look at some specific physical challenges wherein you are probably experiencing mixed feelings about the reality of your growing baby and the drain on your poor, tired body.

MIXED FEELINGS ON WEIGHT GAIN AND BODY SHAPE

So you are gaining weight. Wonderful! Your baby is growing. You're gaining weight. AGHHHH! The scale is reaching new

heights and somehow all of this weight will have to be dealt with once the baby is born. Both of these statements are truths of your pregnant situation and a cause for mixed feelings.

You may be having the same reaction about your growing belly. It is a beautiful sign of the strengthening of your baby and at the same time, it is a bizarre transformation of your once-familiar form. There is a story of a young, pregnant woman who at twenty weeks naively asked, "How much bigger can I get?"

Her midwife had her lie down on the examining table and opened up the paper tape used to measure pregnant women's bellies. She extended the tape from one to forty centimeters (a centimeter for each week of pregnancy) and anchored one end at the top of her pubic bone. Then she brought the other end up and rested it on her sternum. The young pregnant woman saw the ballooning tape before her. Her reaction was shocked silence as she took in the reality of the physical change before her. It is incredible. Your stomach can stick out a foot or more in front of the rest of your body.

Some things you can do when faced with mixed feelings about your increasing body mass are to:

➤ Talk openly about what you are feeling. You don't have to play the sweet pregnant woman. If it is feeling uncomfortable, tell it like it is.

➤ Expect that your body will be, in some way, forever different than it was before you were pregnant. Not doing this can easily build frustration towards yourself and your hardworking body when neither seems to be measuring up to those old standards.

➤ Keep your eating binges to a controlled minimum and commit to eating so you stay within your healthcare provider's recommended weight gain limits. You don't burn calories any differently now that you are pregnant, so everything you eat will either get used up as energy in activities such as building the baby and transporting your growing body or be stored for later use. Don't make pregnancy a time when you increase your fat reserves unnecessarily.

➤ Find a maternity outfit in which you feel good and hang it neatly in your closet. It doesn't need to be expensive. You could find it at a consignment shop, or it could be something lent to you by a friend. But it must be one you put on and in which you feel good. The point here is to take the time to identify that outfit, have all of the pieces together and then put it on every time you feel trapped in a frumpy, uncomfortable, pregnant body.

Mixed Feelings at Bedtime

The concept of sleep poses an interesting challenge during pregnancy. Your body is in need of more sleep than ever before, and at the same time, attempting to sleep can lead to some of the most uncomfortable moments of pregnancy. There can be backaches and sore hips, swollen nasal passages or a foot pressing into your rib cage. If none of these sounds familiar to you, count yourself as fortunate and enjoy the luxury of peaceful slumber. Tanya brings a bit of humor into her sleepless experience of pregnancy.

I am only eighteen weeks pregnant and sleeping is already proving somewhat challenging. Actually, to be totally honest, I began having trouble sleeping as early as eight or nine weeks, but it seemed so ridiculous I could hardly admit it to anyone. My belly didn't rest in my body the way it used to, and I found myself moving from position to position, trying to get comfortable. I wanted to press my belly into myself, almost like I wanted to hold my uterus close. But sleeping and holding your uterus in place doesn't work so well. Luckily, thanks to my cooperative husband, I found if I snuggled up tight against his backside, it had the same effect, placing a support or slight pressure upon my changing body.

Once I fall asleep, I have an array of vivid dreams. They are stumbling over one another, one after the other. I have heard many pregnant women speak of this intriguing side effect of pregnancy, so I know it is normal. But all of these dreams feel so very real, and the odd thing is that, so far, a lot of them are about sex and none of them is about pregnancy or babies. My waking moments are just the opposite — leaving my husband wishing a few of my nighttime dreams would come true.

The next disruption hindering my sleep is those routine trips to the bathroom. It is not that I have to go very often, just a pre-dictable once per night, but the sensation has changed. Instead of waking up with the urgent message, "Get up and pee right now," I am used to receiving in the middle of the night, the message is more like, "Huh, I am awake. Let's see if I can feel the baby moving. So what is the meaning of life anyway? Hey, you know, I think the reason I am awake is because I might need to go to the bathroom." I imagine this bodily confusion is because things have rearranged so much in my body that my bladder doesn't know what it is feeling anymore. It's as if my growing uterus has thrown off the calibration on my internal urination sensor.

Then, in addition to holding up my uterus and trying to recognize if I need to pee or not, I am subject to an extreme case of nightime itching.* I am itchy all over. And once I have gotten up for my nightly pee, I can't fall back to sleep because I am continually scratching myself. Just when I get quieted down, another part of my body begins to itch again. It's my ear, and then a minute later it is my scalp. Then a hair tickles my face. I finally get all of the itching taken care of, and I'm drifting off. Then it is my stomach or my knee or my arm, and the itching starts all over again.

While I am scratching myself back to sleep, I am also tossing and turning, trying to find a comfortable position. I try one side then the other, when what I want to do is lie flat on my back or spread eagle on my stomach. But I've read that both of those positions can be bad for the baby. So I try very hard not to end up on either my front or my back. But I am so tired and uncomfortable. I try to get away with lying just partway on my back. Or I lie on my stomach with part of my body, a leg or a shoulder, turned to one side or another. But neither of these positions seems to work — plus I am left worrying about the baby. Finally, I give up and lie back onto my left side.

All this gets even worse when I wake up in the middle of the night, only to discover the traumatic fact that I have been sleeping on my back for some unknown amount of time. My mind begins screaming, "Roll over! Roll over! Is the baby okay? Did I hurt it at all? Is it getting enough oxygen?" And with that rude awakening, I get to start the whole itching process all over again.

Finally, as if anything can add to all this, it is winter where I live, and that means it is dry. With that added complication, my pregnant body has become a sponge that is forever thirsty, and every ounce of water seems to be going to the baby and its sack of fluids. This has left little moisture for my own poor, host body. I am waking up parched, unable to breathe, with a completely nonfunctional nose and mouth. Both are as dry as newsprint.

*Report any extreme constant itchiness to your medical caregiver.

Nighttime has turned into a three-ring circus. I dread bedtime, but I also know I would endure it all ten times over again to have a healthy baby in my arms at the end of this pregnancy.

If you are facing some of the these discomforts while trying to attain your much-needed rest, take some action to help yourself out by:

➤ Tucking yourself into bed with special care. Pamper yourself with a routine that supports you and the changing needs of your body. This could include taking a relaxing shower just before bed, indulging your senses with some aromathrapy, going for a quiet walk or reading something peaceful.

➤ Anticipating the physical challenges you are likely to experience in the night and staging your night table so you are prepared to address each one without too much midnight activity or commotion. This will allow you to fall back to sleep more easily after each interruption.

➤ Getting creative to make nighttime work for both you and your partner. This could mean upgrading to a bigger bed, staggering your bedtimes or, after a heartfelt goodnight, saying "Au revoir" as your partner heads down the hall to take up residence in the guestroom.

If all else fails, include frequent napping in your daily routine.

MIXED FEELINGS ON MATERNITY CLOTHES

Many women have mixed feelings on maternity clothes. You're dying to wear them, but once you have them on, you are dying to get them off. Claire has something to say about this that you may be able to relate to if you are in the early stages of your pregnancy, or it may be a good reminder of how special this time is if you are towards the end of your pregnancy and feel like you never want to see another item of maternity clothing again in your life.

I am four weeks along with my first child, and given my current size, it is clearly far too early for me to begin looking at maternity clothes. But just for fun, while I was Christmas shopping one day, I stepped into a beautiful maternity store to have a look around.

While I was looking, one of the sales clerks in the shop asked if she could help me. I quickly said no. What was I doing in this store? I felt like some pregnant woman wanna-be. I was pregnant, but I didn't need maternity clothes yet. I hadn't grown an inch and what if I had a miscarriage, then what would I do with maternity clothes? But I was drawn to the store like a moth to a flame. I couldn't help myself. I just wanted to daydream about wearing all of these clothes over my bulging baby belly. I want to imagine myself in one of these beautiful outfits, a sophisticated pregnant woman with a strong healthy baby growing inside.

Right now, I cannot wait for my body to get big. I can't wait to have another piece of clothing be too small for me. I want to just get these small-body pants into someone else's closet. I want to begin looking pregnant. I can't wait to pull on big stretchy panels of spandex or drape folds of flowery print material over my outlandish belly. Bring on the smocks — I want the world to know I'm pregnant.

So if you are early in your pregnancy and dying to wear maternity clothes, do it! Who cares if they are still a bit big. Have some fun with it. If you are late in your pregnancy and dying to get out of maternity clothes, use these three principles to make your remaining tenure within their seams more palatable.

➤ First and foremost, don't leave the house in something that is uncomfortable. If you are beginning to outgrow your maternity clothes, stop wearing them and get some larger, better fitting items for yourself. Again, these can be on loan from a friend or from a consignment shop, so you don't need to spend a lot of money. The key point is that you are comfortable and not feeling constrained by your clothing.

➤ Second, look for ways to refresh these stale clothes you have been wearing over and over for the past months. This could be done by adding a new scarf, swapping a few garments with a pregnant friend or buying a couple new items.

➤ Finally, remind yourself that these are the last few days, weeks or months you will be wearing your maternity clothes. Think about what outfits you like and make sure you wear them often. Enjoy them as much as you can. You won't be using them after your baby is born.

MIXED FEELINGS ON YOUR REPRODUCTIVE SYSTEM

Boy, does this part of your body create mixed feelings and gain some added respect during pregnancy. It goes from being a silent background player to one of the central focuses of your life. Between the needs of your baby and the shifts in your body, you may find you experience all kinds of mixed feelings about this new relationship with your reproductive system. Following are some of the experiences women talk about.

A Newfound Admiration for the Power of Your Uterus. Your uterus, containing your baby and all of its necessary accompaniments, is a muscle that is able to stretch and grow to over forty-five times its normal size, pull itself so it is paper thin and still squeeze the baby out with a force of more than fifty pounds of pressure. Now that is a muscle to stand up and notice! When you find yourself concerned about your uterus, remember that it is normal for your uterus to contract throughout your entire pregnancy, it is simply practicing for labor. However, make sure you are aware of the signs of preterm labor so you can seek medical help if needed. No matter what pain or anxiety your uterus gives you through your pregnancy, respect this muscle and all it is doing for you and your baby by giving it the rest and fluids it needs to do its job.

Prayers for Your Cervix (the opening of your uterus). When else besides during pregnancy do you even take much notice of your cervix let alone pray about it? But during pregnancy, your cervix becomes the controlling force determining your baby's stay inside your body. A cervix that stays closed keeps the baby in. A cervix that opens up too far lets the baby out. It has become a key player in protecting your child's well-being, and you must do everything in your power, including prayer, to keep it closed. On the flipside, once you are in labor, you're dying for the darn thing to open — and fast. If you are having mixed feelings or concerns about the dilation of your cervix, call your healthcare provider. Do not try checking it yourself, doing so can introduce bacteria into the cervix and possibly harm your baby. Finally, let go and realize you cannot control your cervix. Look over the chapter on control and identify what you can do to live comfortably with the unknown actions of this critical part of your body.

Shocked About Your Breasts. As you already know, your breasts will likely have begun metamorphosing before you even have a confirmation that you are pregnant, and they continue to evolve all throughout the pregnancy. Some things that can lead to initial breast shock are their tenderness, their new voluptuous size or their leaking colostrum. All of this can cause mixed feelings for you and your partner. One very helpful way to manage such mixed feelings is to take on an attitude of gentleness towards your breasts. They are going through a lot right now, preparing to do the job for which they were designed. Protect them from jarring motion or uncomfortable positions. Try wearing a comfortable bra to bed at night. This provides some additional support and prevents your breasts from rubbing against clothing or bed sheets, which only increases their tenderness. You should also stop into a maternity shop and request a sales clerk assist you in finding several bras that fit well. Do the same to prepare for nursing if that is a choice you have made. A well-fitting bra can make a big difference now as well as after the baby is born.

Having Sex ... or Not. No doubt about it, you can count on this aspect of your physical life to change during your pregnancy, sometimes for better and sometimes for worse. Either way, it's different in ways you cannot even imagine. Many women come into their doctor's office and complain that their partners don't want to have sex with them now that they are pregnant. The common line sounds something like this, "Finally, I can have sex without worrying I will get pregnant, and he doesn't want to because he is afraid he'll hurt the baby." Or, the opposite happens, your partner is even more attracted to your pregnant body, and you don't feel anything close to sexy ... in fact attempting sex of any kind is the last thing of which you want any part. To bridge these mixed up feelings, be frank and honest with your partner regarding how you feel about sex. You can get creative in how you go about meeting each other's needs for intimacy. And definitely do whatever is needed to reassure your partner that sex will not hurt the baby. For more information on this topic, see Strategy Eight: Find Your Way to Gentleness with Your Spouse.

Awakening Past Traumas. For some women, having so much

attention focused on their reproductive systems can lead to very negative feelings. It can be common for women who have experienced any kind of sexual abuse to find themselves reconnecting with old pain or fears during this time of pregnancy and delivery. These past experiences can complicate pregnancy or labor. If this is a potential reality for you, take some proactive steps to get some support and assistance by talking with your healthcare provider or a trained counselor.

Mixed Feelings with the Functioning of Your Brain

If all that is not enough, even your brain functioning can be temporarily impaired. Now you have mixed thoughts on top of your mixed feelings. Sounds like the beginnings of a personal pan of scrambled eggs. But it is true. A team of British researchers, led by Anita Holdcroft, M.D., scanned the brains of ten women using magnetic resonance imaging and found their brains were physically smaller during pregnancy than they were at six months after delivery. Not by a lot, mind you, but this and other studies have uncovered that the brains of pregnant women do shrink and cognitive functioning is altered. Ann had something to say about this experience.

I could tell my sharp eye and quick wit were slightly dulled quite early in my pregnancy, but I had no idea what this was about or what was going on. Then I read an article about the shrinking brains of pregnant women. Yes, apparently it is a proven fact that the brains of pregnant women do shrink, just enough to leave you doing all kinds of ridiculous things.

I began my shrinking-brain syndrome early on in my pregnancy, at about four weeks. I locked my keys in my car with the engine running. This was quite embarrassing! I was already late for a meeting, and now I had to explain to these people, who hardly knew me, what I had done. Then I had to take up more of our meeting time getting my car door open and the engine turned off. Thankfully, the mechanic who arrived to break into my running car was very polite about the whole thing, although I think I am glad I didn't get to hear what he told the guys back at the garage. Twenty dollars and thirty minutes later, it was all over, and I could focus my slightly smaller brain on the topics of my meeting.

With my ever-shrinking brain, I am also finding I have trouble remembering the names of people I know very well. Just like the car key incident, this is also quite embarrassing. Sometimes it happens with my good friends; other times it is with work colleagues. I feel like I just can't bring these very familiar names to the surface. To be honest, I have never been good at remembering people's names, but this is getting ridiculous. I have forgotten the names of people I have known for years. I guess the upside is now I can blame this long-running social faux pas on my pregnancy.

So far, I have managed this shrinking-brain thing well enough to keep my job, and I seem to be functioning at an adequate, or at least safe, level in my home. My only hope is that there is no correlation between the growth of my stomach and shrinking of my brain. If so, I fear for the lives of those around me in the coming nine months.

Locking your keys in the car seems to be a very common pregnancy experience. To avoid this and the many other possible brainless actions you could take:

- ➤ Make lists to help you remember the critical things you must not forget.
- ➤ Slow down and take time to double check, do I have my keys? Do I have everything I need?
- ➤ Create backup systems for yourself, such as carrying a spare key or having a co-worker look over some of your more complex projects.
- ➤ Finally, as a last resort, consider the help of modern conveniences such as setting an alarm to remind you of an important appointment or keyless entry for your car.

MIXED FEELINGS ON OTHERS' COMMENTS ABOUT YOUR BODY

One final place you may find yourself experiencing mixed feelings is in the comments others may make about your body. Sometimes these comments can be wonderful. People notice you so much more when you are pregnant, and they cannot help but tell you how beautiful you look, or they offer to be helpful in so many different ways. They all want to do what they can to be a part of providing support for you and your unborn baby.

If you are a new parent, another fun reaction you can get from others is that dreamy eyed look when you tell them this will be your first child. They seem to be instantly transported to all the positive feelings of being pregnant with their first child and they sigh like people do when they think of the first time they fell in love.

On the flipside, people can also say some very unhelpful things. They can stress how large you are, as if you don't already know, leaving you even more aware of your tent-like qualities. They can jump immediately into a story about their own pregnancy and go on for quite some time with something that has little or nothing to do with you. Or, even worse, they can tell you the latest horror that just might happen to you given your current situation.

You just never know what to expect when someone you don't know lights up at the sight of your pregnancy. So, take pleasure in bringing out the best in some and learn to tactfully interrupt others. Some strategies for creating a needed interruption are to:

> Make a funny statement that catches them off guard and stops them cold.
> Excuse yourself and go to the bathroom.
> Take a step back when they reach for your stomach, and change the subject or politely ask them not to touch you. (If this hasn't already happened to you, count yourself as lucky. For some reason, a segment of the population is overtaken with this indescribable need to touch the belly of any pregnant woman they see. For some pregnant women this is no big deal, but for others it can feel invasive. With most, the intent is not to invade. Instead, it is about the magnetism of the miracle of life. There is something so wonderful and miraculous about pregnancy that people are drawn to it like little else in life, causing them to rub your stomach and break with all commonly established social norms. Do what you need to feel comfortable with this odd social phenomenon.)

If employing these kinds of interruptions is a challenge for you at first, practice them with your partner or a friend.

Tools for Living with (and Maybe even Resolving) These Mixed Feelings About Your Body

Let's give you some tools to successfully traverse this time of change and mixed feelings about your body. Below is a diverse set of tools to ease your body-based mental turmoil and bring you some well-deserved comfort and peace of mind. Pick out those tools you think will work the best for you. Choose those you are drawn to and that may bring a bit of relief or a burst of fun to the physical and emotional challenges of residing in your pregnant body.

Tool Number One: Name Your Pain

There is so much changing within your body it can feel like every part is crying for attention. You can get bogged down and distracted when you feel that everything is broken. If this is the case for you, it might help to name your specific pain. By sitting down and identifying your specific ailments or uncovering exactly what is changing, you can release this overwhelming total body breakdown and focus your energy on the few parts of your body that need the attention, all of which lightens your load.

An additional benefit may be some gratitude in finding a whole list of ailments you are not currently feeling. Maybe you get to finish this excercise feeling significantly more fortunate than you did before you started.

Use the list below to assist you with this process. Identify the specific parts of your body that are feeling some discomfort, circle the ailments you are experiencing, as well as how that ailment affects you. Then, read some of the common causes for discomfort in this part of the body, which are in your sphere of control, and choose those causes that may address your discomfort. Now you have something to try that might bring relief.

There will be discomforts you have no power to change. Those you will just have to live with. But you have nothing to lose in trying something; it is always worth a shot. Use these suggestions to assist you in taking some action to alleviate your discomfort, but before you do anything, it is critical you call and talk it over with your healthcare provider.

Head
THE AILMENT
Ache
Tired
Dizzy
Fainting
Nose bleeding
Increased salivation
Drymouth
Other _____

HOW IT AFFECTS YOU
Leaves you feeling tired
Feel mentally slowed down
Unable to focus
Uncomfortable
Scares you
Other _____

*COMMON CAUSES WITHIN YOUR CONTROL
Not enough water
Lack of sleep
Tension or anxiety
Low blood sugar, needing to eat
Lack of vitamin C
Low humidity level in home
Standing too long
Lack of iron

Neck
THE AILMENT
Sore
Stiff
Ache
Tension
Other _____

HOW IT AFFECTS YOU
Annoys you
Distracts you

Limits your ability to turn your head

Hurts

Other _____

*COMMON CAUSES WITHIN YOUR CONTROL

Sleeping without the proper support.

Sitting in a ergonomically incorrect chair at work

Poor posture

Back
THE AILMENT

Ache

Stiff

Sore

Uncomfortable

Other _____

HOW IT AFFECTS YOU

Limits your ability to move or exercise

Makes you want to hold up your pregnant belly

Hurts

Other _____

*COMMON CAUSES WITHIN YOUR CONTROL

Sleeping on an old mattress (lumpy, saggy, unsupportive)

Lifting heavy things, such as an older child

Wearing improper shoes

Maintaining an uncomfortable sitting or standing position for
     long periods of time

Too much or too little exercise

Skipping a helpful massage

Breasts
THE AILMENT

Sore

Ache

Nipple tenderness

Leaking colosterum

Hurts

Other _____

How it Affects You

Leaves you feeling tired

Leaves you feeling physically or emotionally vulnerable

Limits your activity

Other _____

*Common Causes Within Your Control

Wearing a bra that no longer fits

Forgetting to wear a form of light breast support while sleeping

Your Pregnant Belly
The Ailment

Tight

Itchy skin

Bloated

Frequently spilling food on your belly

Other _____

How it Affects You

Slows you down

Feel unsteady on your feet or clumsy

Hurts

Uncomfortable pressure

Ruins the few maternity clothes you like

Other _____

*Common Causes Within Your Control

Lack of moisture in the skin, needing lotion

Clothes that are too tight around the waist

Lack of vitamin C or E for the skin

Eating too many peppers, onions, beans, brussel sprouts,
or broccoli

Eating too much food at any one time

Stomach
The Ailment

Sore

Nauseous

Indigestion

Vomiting

Constipation

Gas Pain

Other _____

How it Affects You

Stops you in your tracks

Scares you

Leaves you feeling sick

Limits how you can live your life

Other _____

*Common Causes Within Your Control

Not eating enough food

Not eating small amounts every two hours throughout the day

Eating incorrect types of food

Not drinking enough fluids

Pelvis

The Ailment

Sharp Pains

Loose joints

Hemorrhoids

Other _____

How it Affects You

Scares you

Uncomfortable

Painful

Other _____

*Common Causes Within Your Control

Forgetting to maintain good body posture when lifting

Too little time off your feet, try a warm bath or shower

Pressure from the weight of the belly, try a maternity
    brace or belt

Legs

The Ailment

Cramps

Aching legs

Lose your balance

Feeling unstable

Other _____

How it Affects You

Painful

Keeps you up at night

Uncomfortable

Other _____

***Common Causes Within Your Control**

A calcium imbalance, either too much or too little

Lying on your back

Too much or too little activity

Maintaining one position for too long

Ankles and Feet

The Ailment

Swollen

Wobbly

Sore

Other _____

How it Affects You

Unsteady on your feet

Uncomfortable

Pant cuffs, socks or shoes feel too tight

Other _____

***Common Causes Within Your Control**

Too much salt in your diet and not enough protein

Sitting in a chair for too long without getting up and
changing positions

Letting your legs dangle off the edge of a chair or table rather
than supporting them in an elevated position

Wearing clothing or shoes that are too small

* While all of these common causes are a good place to start,
it is critical that you also talk with your healthcare provider
about the specific symptoms and solutions for each of your
physical challenges.

Now, look back at your list and see what is happening to your
body. Are you less overwhelmed by all of these physical challenges
now that you can see it all in black and white? Do you notice any

trends? What are you doing to exacerbate your current list of physical ailments? It can be interesting to go through this same body assessment two or three months further into your pregnancy and see what changes have taken place or which new physical challenges you face.

TOOL NUMBER TWO: SEE YOUR BODY FROM A NEW PERSPECTIVE

For most women, the perspective, or way they look at their changing bodies can have a big impact on the mixed feelings attached to all this physical change. Let's take a look at some of the more helpful perspectives you can hold about your changing body.

Your body as the most beautiful science project ever! When you think about it, your body is undergoing quite a scientific feat. Most of your past scientific feats were conducted with old Bunsen burners, frogs or small white mice, reeking of formaldehyde, and required spending time with a lab partner you may not have been

all that excited about. But now, your project, creating life, is occurring within this beautiful and sophisticated collection of cells, your body. Any accompanying smells are those you've chosen — for the most part — and on most days you're crazy in love with your lab partner. To top if all off, your tiny newborn creation is equally lovely. It is all enough to make Dr. Frankenstein green with envy!

Your physical changes as temporary. Many of the changes affecting your body are temporary. They will last for up to nine months and then change again, maybe snapping back more or less in place or metamorphosing a second time into a new postpregnant body. When you are distressed over your physical changes, continue to remind yourself that many of these body changes are not permanent, even if they may feel like it at the time.

Your body as an organic process. Much of our society has done an overly effective job of setting up women to strive for a set of extremely unrealistic body standards. This is no news to any of you; you see it every day. But as you also know all too well, bodies are not made to fit into anybody else's standards, each is made unique, and pregnancy will have a unique impact on each body. The point is that bodies are much more of an ever-changing process than an instrument meeting a set of standard measurements. Year by year, bodies are made to shift and change as we go through all of the activities in our lives. Pregnancy, with its physical drama, just makes us more aware of it. Bodies are alive and dynamic, and the reality is that with some healthy habits, either in or out of pregnancy, each body looks just as it is supposed to.

Your body as something to care for. We often think about our bodies serving us or being a tool to serve us, but what if we reversed that relationship and looked instead at the body as something you are caring for or serving? How does that change the perspective you have on your pregnant body? What can you take from this perspective to help you traverse all of the personal transitions involved in the physical changes of pregnancy? This perspective could increase your ability to be gentle with your body. It could enable you to let go of some of the demands you have on your body or release some of the expectations you have about its performance. It could open you up to the interdependence you truly have with this vessel that is carrying you around on the earth. Maybe it could even free you to see your body as a different entity from yourself, an important part of you, but only one piece of what makes you a complete person.

Your body as a part of a miracle. Many women and their partners get caught up in the new lumpiness or the aches and pains of pregnancy and forget to notice the fact that this is their time to participate in the miracle of life. Right now, your body is doing some of the most amazing work it will ever do. Nobody really understands how it performs this awesome feat. What turns this mass of cells into a beating heart? How do your cells know to form a heart or a spinal column or legs? And how does the body know when it is the right time to push out the baby ? Even though you may be feeling less than wonderful, for your body, this is a peak experience. What is it like to be in awe of your body with all of its accompanying lumps and bumps?

Your body as a path to intimacy with your baby. While you are pregnant, you have the opportunity to experience a physical intimacy with your baby that will end once he or she is born and the two of you are separate individuals. This is the one time in your lives together that you will have this child physically attached to you. Much of the future is about growing up and away. But now, while you are pregnant, it is a time of physical interdependence. Kate describes this opportunity for intimacy with her unborn child very clearly.

We are thirty-five weeks pregnant, and I feel great. In fact, I can tell that I will actually miss not being pregnant. Like right now, the baby has the hiccups. This is the second time in twelve hours, and they are strong enough that my whole stomach is moving with each hiccup. This and all the other sensations are so incredible. I can sit and stare out the window for long periods of time, just feeling the baby move. When I wake up in the middle of the night, I put my hands on my tummy to feel it moving. If I haven't noticed it moving in awhile, I find a quiet place to sit and wait until it moves, to ensure it is still okay. I like this little person moving around inside of me.

I realize I will miss not having this little baby inside of me, and when I tell this to others they often respond by saying, "Oh, but you'll have this new person to be with out in the world." Like they need to help me see that there is nothing to miss. But they are terribly wrong, and I already know it. I will be ecstatic to have my baby in my arms, and at the same time I will miss carrying him or her in the deepest part of my body.

It's not that I am complaining or worrying. It is more that I want to soak up this time as much as possible because it will be gone so soon. I want to appreciate and enjoy it because soon this baby will be out of my body and this magical thing happening between the two of us will be over. I am sure another amazing thing happens as my husband and I begin to learn to be parents to this child, but it will be very different from now. And I can never get now back again.

Your body is providing this baby with the perfect home. Every place you go, you have your baby right there with you, and you don't have to share it with anyone else in the world. It is just between the two of you. What is it like for you to have this child so close? Think about it for a moment. What does that mean for you and how does it feel?

Each of these very different perspectives on your changing body contains some truth about you and your pregnancy. Choose one that will serve you right now. Use them all throughout your pregnancy to keep you clear on what matters in the midst of so much physical change.

TOOL NUMBER THREE: DO SOMETHING NEW OR DIFFERENT!

Your body is doing something outrageous, growing a baby and dramatically changing shape. What if you did something outrageous in response? Nothing dangerous to you or your baby, but something that allowed you to explore or play a bit with what is happening to you. For example, you could:

➤ Check out an alternative method of preparing for labor.

➤ Dress your pregnant body up in a wild costume, which allowed your belly to show and take some pictures of yourself. (The book *Pregnant Goddesshood*, listed in the reference section of this chapter, has some great examples of this.)

➤ Get a large piece of packaging paper, as big as your own body, lie down on it, and have your partner trace the profile of your changed body. This would be most interesting if done close to your due date, or you could lie in the same spot once during each month of your pregnancy and see the changes taking place over time.

➤ Make a plaster cast of your belly and hang it in your baby's room, paint it or fill it with flowers.

➤ Hire a photographer to take a beautiful picture of your pregnant body.

➤ Write a glowing description of all of the changes taking place in your body. For example, you could think about the new stretch marks crawling across your belly and write: "I feel the tingling of stretch marks burn across my belly. They seem to be circling my belly button like the arms of a distant spinning solar system. To augment this cosmic theme, I have considered following the fashion trend of a popular Star Trek character and have the stretch lines died black." Now that is a new way of looking at stretch marks. Where else can you create something a bit outrageous for yourself?

Tool Number Four: Write Your Own Body Guidelines

Whether you have ever thought about it or not, most of us subscribe to a set of guidelines about our body. These are the standard routines you follow, how you eat, exercise or dress. They are the ideas you have about what you need to do to care for your body, as well as expectations you maintain for your body. Pregnancy is a perfect time to rewrite the guidelines you set for your body. You may want to add some new rules, take away some or just slightly alter the ones to which you currently subscribe. Some intriguing guidelines to consider adding are:

➤ Treating yourself to something small, but special, on some kind of a daily or weekly basis.

➤ Committing to only eat foods you like.

➤ Cleaning out your closet and keeping only the clothing that you feel good wearing.

➤ Finding exercise options that you consider fun, such as yoga, a dance class or water aerobics.

➤ Starting to eat breakfast again.

➤ Committing to get enough sleep every night.

➤ Starting or stoping wearing makeup, shaving a part of your body or wearing certain jewelry.

➤ What self-imposed guidelines could you change and improve the quality of your pregnancy?

Tool Number Five: Listen and Respond to Your Body's Needs

By now, you have seen this concept at least a couple of times, and you will find it at least a couple more times before you are finished reading this book. This redundancy is intentional. Listening and responding to your body's needs is one of the best things you can do to take care of yourself, and, for many, it comes in last place behind all of the other demands of life. All of you, your body, mind and spirit are the core of what you have to offer yourself and your new baby. Take good care of all parts of you so they will be strong when you and your baby need them. Only you know exactly what it means to listen and respond to the needs of your body, mind and spirit, but let's look at some common areas to consider.

Caring for Your Body

➤ Relax and learn some techniques to minimize your tendency to get stressed out.

➤ Eat foods that sound fulfilling and leave you feeling physically good as your body digests them.

➤ Sleep as much as it takes to wake up feeling refreshed.

Caring for Your Mind

➤ Read books that nourish, restore and replenish your mind.

➤ Take a quiet moment to get realigned with the thoughts, opinions and ideas swimming through your own head.

➤ Try new things. Eat a new kind of ethnic food, take a class in something about which you know nothing or explore a public park to which you have never been before.

Caring for Your Heart

➤ Reflect on those things that are important to you.

➤ Be sure you are taking enough time to spend with the people you care about.

➤ Don't make yourself do anything that you know you don't want to do.

Consider how you could apply all of these strategies to your pregnant life. Then do yourself and your body a favor, pick one action that you will commit to doing in the coming week.

When the Body Challenge Increases: Living with Significant Physical Limitations

Lots of these body changes are annoying but tolerable. Then there are the real showstoppers, things like morning sickness and bedrest. It is virtually impossible to maintain life-as-usual while in the throes of either one. Whether for one week or nine months, both morning sickness and bedrest can dramatically change how you live your life for that period of time and beyond.

With that said, don't make either of these an additional worry you add to your list. Neither condition is much fun, but both are survivable, and you will get through either one if it becomes a part of your pregnancy. Instead, the focus here is on supporting those who are currently facing the personal challenges each condition can bring.

THE REAL SCOOP ON ... FLUSH ... MORNING SICKNESS

Unfortunately, for many pregnant women, the toilet bowl becomes a very familiar sight. Maria experienced a mild case of morning sickness in both of her pregnancies, and was shocked at the punch it could pack.

As a female in this society, I'd heard about morning sickness throughout my whole life. It is the common experience of the stereotypical pregnant woman and often the brunt of many a sit-com joke. Before experiencing it, I thought morning sickness was kind of sweet, a clear sign of the wonderful life growing inside. Ha! What a fairy tale that is. When I got pregnant, I had no idea what I was in for.

I was shocked when I felt the initial clutch of morning sickness take hold of me. It was not at all what I had imagined. I had even read many of the standard pregnancy books, and they all made morning sickness sound like a mild irritation. Maybe, medically, it's no big deal. But when you are living with it day in and day out, morning sickness is huge. It is this relentless, unimaginable awfulness that lasts up to twenty-four hours a day. For those of you without any firsthand experience, it feels like there is some giant, dead fish rotting inside your body.

I wish someone had told me what morning sickness was like so I could have prepared myself. I could have set my expectations more in line with reality and not been so shocked when this "no-big-deal" event so dramatically changed my lifestyle.

To accentuate this shock, people who are further along in their pregnancy seem to just forget about how yucky morning sickness is. Mercifully for them, nature seems to arrange that all of these memories just shrink away as quickly as your stomach grows. However, unfortunately for me, currently trapped in its clutches, nobody seems to remember how bad it was. The net result of all of this is, as a woman in the throes of morning sickness, I was left feeling both desperately ill and quite alone.

If morning sickness is a part of your pregnancy, step back and accept the fact that, for the most part, you have no direct control over when or how to feel better. There are millions of things to try — and try them all — some may work for a while and some may not — but basically you are in a time of just existing through what is a taxing, but temporary, state until the nausea passes. At least accepting this will keep you from continuing to bang your head on the wall thinking this could all be better if only you could unlock the mystery of why you feel so rotten. It is a very consuming experience, and it normally has an impact on every part of you, limiting your ability to enjoy your pregnancy or anything else.

BEDREST

Tina had a very unusual and dramatic experience with bedrest and was able to speak very thoughtfully about it. She was on bedrest for seven months. So, for three seasons within the year of her pregnancy, she was either lying on her couch or in her bed. This experience was so extreme, it changed her forever. But even a short confinement to bedrest can change your whole sense of self. If bedrest of any length is a challenge you are now facing, you may find some pearls of wisdom here in Tina's reflections.

The two biggest emotions I remember when I found out I would be on bedrest for a long period of time were fear and being overwhelmed. I had no idea how I would do bedrest for seven months. I was so afraid for my baby. Overall, I can honestly say I was downright terrified. Slowly, those initial emotions evolved into acceptance and, though I still had worries about not being able to control the outcome, I began to see that I did have a small piece of control in all of this. I could do what I was supposed to, as instructed by my doctor. By strictly following this regime – I was doing the best thing I could to care for this baby growing inside of me.

The first thing I noticed while on bedrest was how much help I needed and how hard it was to ask for it. Now, when I say hard, it's not like I sat there agonizing about whether to pick up the phone and call someone to help me. No, what was hard was just realizing I needed to get others help. I was used to doing things for myself, not asking for help. So the thought never crossed my mind and I didn't ever ask — neither did my husband. We just limped along doing the best we could in an extremely challenging situation. I am a lot wiser now, and if I am ever on bedrest again, I am going to set up help for myself right away. I am going to put those that offer on a schedule for bringing meals to us, and I am going to ask people to take me to some of my doctor appointments.

The next thing I saw creeping into my life was isolation, and it didn't make a lot of sense to me at the time. I had lots of visitors and people around me, and at the same time, I felt very alone with this whole bedrest challenge. People just didn't get what it meant to be on bedrest. They couldn't understand why I wasn't able to come to that special family dinner or why I didn't just sit back and enjoy this time of being free to read a whole day away.

And, as strange as it sounds, it was actually hard for me to have visitors. They often came with so much energy and enthusiasm; it was just too overwhelming. I felt jittery from the medication I was taking, and it was hard to focus on what they were saying. I always wanted to have my husband present to interact with them.

So, I spent much of my bedrest time alone. I slept a lot and read a bit, although my medication made both of those activities challenging as well. I did needlepoint projects and watched movies. I imagined this is what life must be like for those who are terminally ill, only I knew no matter what the outcome, it would end at forty weeks or sooner, and I would probably still be around when it was all over.

My time on bedrest was also a huge life change for my husband. Not only did he have to do all — think about it — all of the chores around the house, as well as take care of me, but I was no longer the woman he had married. During my time on bedrest, I had changed in every conceivable way. The balance of power in our relationship was totally thrown off, there was no such thing as romance and he had to just continue picking up the slack. To say it was a strain on our marriage is putting it lightly.

Finally, the residual impact of bedrest, after the baby was born, totally caught me by surprise. We all believed that once the baby came everything would go back to normal. However, that was far from the case. Not only did I have the usual transition of learning how to care for a newborn and becoming a mom, I had to relearn how to function as something other than a couch-bound, human incubator. I was not used to having activity in my life. I was emotionally overwhelmed, and I had to relearn many of the basics, such as how to drive. When I came home from the hospital with my newborn son, it took me at least another nine months to get myself back up to speed.

If you are currently facing a significant physical limitation such as morning sickness or bedrest in your pregnancy, you know all too well the powerful changes it can bring about in your life. Now it is no longer about planning and accomplishing, but instead the focus is on getting through the day.

For many women, pregnancy is the first time they have ever experienced the effects of any real physical limitation. Most of us are used to feeling good and doing what we need to do when we need to do it. If a physical limitation is something you have to manage in your pregnancy, take a couple of moments to provide some support to yourself by considering the following questions:

> ➤ What is the biggest challenge for you in this limitation?
> ➤ How are you responding to this challenge?
> ➤ What part of your response is proving to be unhelpful?
> ➤ What could you do to let go of this part of your response and add something that will enable you to take better care of yourself through this?
> ➤ How do you see yourself changing from this?

It can be helpful to keep a diary with some of these questions and your answers. Take some additional time with those questions that strike a cord or strengthen your peace of mind in this challenging situation. Throughout the pregnancy, both you and your physical limitations are likely to change, thus your responses to these questions will likely continue to change as well. Some changes you could expect are:

> ➤ Easy tasks could become much harder.
> ➤ Things that are hard now and could become a piece of cake later in the pregnancy.
> ➤ Your overall outlook or perspective changes.
> ➤ A change has occurred in another part of your life, such as

leaving your current job, which has a big impact on you and your pregnancy.

By taking a couple of moments to write your responses to the above questions, you will be able to look back and see the shifts that have taken place in you throughout your pregnancy.

Accepting Your Current Reality

During your pregnancy, physical alterations or discomforts may be your reality. Not necessarily a lot of fun, but fighting it is not going to make it better and might even make it worse. The best thing you can do right now is practice personal acceptance of what is. Sounds straightforward, but in fact it can be one of the tougher things to do. Below is a set of three principles to assist you in beginning the process of personally accepting the current reality of your body-based changes. Following these guidelines can be a very useful way to respond to the personal challenges that come with all of your physical changes.

1. GRIPE ABOUT IT

You don't have to be the worst off to complain loudly and often about the physical annoyances you are experiencing. Talking about how it feels can bring you the support of others and minimize that alone feeling. Even a mild physical limitation can feel torturous at times. It can quickly drain you physically, mentally and emotionally.

Whatever the situation about your pregnancy and others' reactions to it, allow yourself the luxury of acknowledging that it feels awful, even if it's only on paper. If you begin griping to someone only to have them tell you it's all worth it or it's not that bad, tell them you are aware of that and you just want some time to talk about it. Then consider the following gripe guidelines to keep you from swinging off on a gripearama:

> ➤ Only tell each person once. You can tell everyone once, but don't start repeating the same gripe over and over.
> ➤ Don't consume the whole conversation with your gripe. Make room to hear what is going on in others' lives as well.
> ➤ Look for the possible humor that might be found in your current gripe.
> ➤ Finally, as a gift to yourself, use these same guidelines to contain the gripes lingering within your own mind.

Taking the opportunity to do a little griping allows you to let go of the burden of your situation. You are admitting to yourself and others that this is a real drag. At the same time, openly sharing your reality will likely get you some well-deserved sympathy and support. It is simple, yet powerful. Life is not always great right now and by doing some griping, you let those around you understand.

2. Stop the Struggle and Start the Acceptance

The next thing you can do to help yourself manage is to simply accept your current plight. It is the simple act of acceptance that will lighten your load through this time and, believe it or not, give you a feeling of personal peace. To do this requires relying on the basic age-old philosophy of "living in the moment."

So, take a deep breath and accept that this is how you will be feeling for however long you feel it. You know the pace, moment by moment, step by step and day by day. Just get through the next couple of minutes and then get through the next couple after that and so on until who knows when. Eventually, these moments will pass. There is nothing fast or fancy about this coping mechanism. It is quiet, focused, disciplined and, in most cases, effective.

I realize this sounds like a bit of a contradiction, talk about how awful it is and then submit to and accept it. But both are necessary and true. It is a very hard time and, unless you want to end the pregnancy, it is what you must go through right now.

You tell people about how it feels for you and then exist with it. Practicing the discipline of living with these two contradictory actions can provide you with both the support you need from the world around you, as well as give you the added internal peace and strength you need to continue living through this challenge.

3. Give into Your Body's Demands

Here it is again — Listen to your body and give it what it needs. Tuning into your own internal needs can take some retraining. Some things to listen for are:

➤ Signs of your body reaching a new limit.
➤ A desire to just go home or go to bed.
➤ Watching for that internal "be polite" voice.
➤ A desire to do something out of the ordinary.

What your body is asking for may not make sense or seem rational or logical at the time. But if you can hear and respond to your body's requests, you will be reducing, if even in a very small way, the disorienting personal effects of all your physical challenges.

For many of us, we are not taught to treat ourselves with such care. We focus all of our attention outward and forget about taking good care of ourselves. Now, as a pregnant woman, it is time to shift that trend. You and your baby both require that you listen to what you need and respond accordingly. And yes, you have commitments and there will be things you have to do even if you don't want to do them. But, at the same time, there is much you can cut out. Give yourself some room to take gentle and loving care of yourself through each of your physical challenges. Pregnancy is not the time to worry about conforming to all of our social norms. Do what you feel is in the best interest of you and your baby — you can leave that party ten minutes after you arrived, even if it does seem a bit outrageous or impolite.

As a pregnant woman, you are learning a whole new way of existing within your body, but the rules keep changing on you. Listen to the changing needs of your body, mind and spirit. Acknowledge yourself for all you have done so far and the courage you have, walking with huge faith into a new life with your baby. Accept the physical challenges contained within this pregnancy and remember that all you can do is your best — and that is more than enough!

Summary

So Whose Body Is this Again?

Body Ups
> ➤ You have a newfound respect for your body and the amazing feats it can perform.
> ➤ With the help of your pregnant point of view, you are able to find acceptance for the long-annoying quirks and foibles of your body.
> ➤ You finally find yourself committing to some important body-based habits you want to maintain far beyond the nine months of your pregnancy.
> ➤ You are the only one on the whole planet who ever gets to experience this kind of complete physical connection with your baby.

Body Downs
> ➤ Your body is making some seriously uncomfortable changes.
> ➤ You have to let go of some of the expectations you have for your body.
> ➤ You have a jumble of mixed up feelings about the changes within your body.
> ➤ A good night's sleep is becoming more and more elusive.
> ➤ You are uncomfortable with how others treat you when they see your pregnant body.
> ➤ You're stuck with the physical, mental and emotional challenges of morning sickness or bedrest.
> ➤ You have to let go of how life used to be in your prepregnant body and figure out how to live within your current physical realities.

RESOURCES

On Sleep

The Promise of Sleep: A Pioneer in Sleep Medicine Explores the Vital Connection Between Health, Happiness and a Good Night's Sleep, Dr. William Dement and Christopher Vauahan. (New York, NY: Dell Books, 2000.)

The Complete Guide to Natural Sleep, Dian Dincin Buchman and Don R. Bensen. (New York, NY: McGraw Hill, 1997.)

American Sleep Disorders Association, www.asda.org
This is a professional association for practitioners focusing on sleep medicine and research.

National Sleep Foundation, www.sleepfoundation.org
This is a nonprofit organization that promotes, educates and conducts research about sleep and the issues that affect sleep. Address: 1522 K Street NW, Suite 510, Washington, DC 20005.

On Breastfeeding

La Leche League International, www.lalecheleague.org
A worldwide organization focused on helping mothers to breastfeed through mother-to-mother support, information and education. Phone: (847) 519-7730
Address: 1400 N. Meacham Rd., Schaumburg, IL 60168-4079

Breastfeeding.com, www.breastfeeding.com
A site for breastfeeding information, support and assistance.

On Body Image

Lit From Within: Tending Your Soul for Lifelong Beauty, Victoria Moran. (San Francisco, CA: Harper San Francisco, 2001.)

The Body Image Workbook: An 8-Step Program for Learning to Like Your Looks, Thomas F. Cash, Ph.D. (New Harbinger Publications, 1997.)

Transforming Body Image: Love the Body You Have, Marcia Germaine Hutchinson. (Freedom, CA: The Crossing Press, 1988.)

On Maternity Clothes

Pregnancy Chic: The Fashion Survival Guide, Cherie Serota and Jody Kozlow Gardner. (Villard Books, 1998.)

Estyle, www.estyle.com
Online shopping for maternity wear, as well as all baby and kid needs.

On Something New and Different
Birthing From Within: An Extraordinary Guide to Childbirth Preparation, Pam England and Rob Horowitz. (Partera Press, 1998.)

Pregnant Goddesshood: A Celebration of Life, Mazy Ann Halpin. (Santa Monica, CA: General Publishing Group, 1997.)

Creative Childbirth: The Leclaire Method of Easy Birthing Through Hypnosis and Rational-Intuitive Thought, Michelle Leclaire O'Neill. (Papyrus Press, 1993.)

On Morning Sickness
No More Morning Sickness: A Survival Guide for Pregnant Women, Mariam Erick. (Plume, 1993.)

Pregnancy Sickness: Using Your Body's Natural Defenses to Protect Your Baby-To-Be, Margie Profet and Mary Kirikorian. (Perseus Press, 1997.)

All of the websites listed in the on pregnancy resources from the first chapter also contain helpful resources on morning sickness.

On Bedrest
Days in Waiting: A Guide to Surviving Pregnancy Bedrest, Mary Ann McCann. (A Place To Remember, 1999.)

When Pregnancy Isn't Perfect: A Layperson's Guide to Complications In Pregnancy, Laurie Rich. (Larata Press, 1996.)

On Acceptance
Succulent Wild Woman: Dancing With Your Wonder Full Self, Sark. (Fireside, 1997.)

Ending the Struggle Against Yourself: A Workbook for Developing Deep Confidence and Self-Acceptance, Stan Taubman. (New York, NY: JP Tarcher, 1994.)

STRATEGY THREE

PARE DOWN COMMITMENTS
TO A LIMITED SET OF PRIORITIES

There is a fairy tale out there, and it is driving many crazy. They have been duped into believing that if they give it just a little more effort, it could be their reality. The tale begins something like this: "If I just work a little harder, plan a little better or cut out that extra fluff in my life, I can have it all. I don't have to make any of those hard choices or let go of anything. I can fit it all into my calendar, all I have to do is sleep less and schedule it all back to back." And although you may physically be able to get your body to all of the places you want it to be, your heart, mind and spirit will be left racing to catch up. Lindsey struggled with this throughout much of her pregnancy.

I was doing what I thought was best. I had so many things that I was committed to before I got pregnant, and I knew that once I had the baby I wouldn't be able to do as much. I just wanted to get everything as organized and caught up as possible.

Through most of my pregnancy, I worked all day, had commitments most evenings and loads of social engagements plus household responsibilities on the weekends. I was exhausted most of my pregnancy. I gained a lot of extra weight because I didn't give myself time to make healthy food. I know it all made getting ready for our baby much harder. My husband and I didn't take the time for just the two of us to enjoy our last months as a couple without children. I didn't get to enjoy my time preparing for the baby; it ended up being just one more item on an overflowing to-do list. And worst of all, I didn't stop long enough to appreciate my pregnancy.

Now, it is over, and I have a beautiful baby girl. I'm definitely slowing down now to spend time with her. I just wish I would have made the shift during my pregnancy. By being so busy, I missed the most important things throughout my nine months of carrying her.

When we try to do it all and put too much into the 24 hours we have each day, something has to give, and oftentimes it ends up being us. Don't allow yourself to live this kind of madness. What is the point of being all of these places and doing all of these things if you're exhausted, crabby or totally stressed out? Set some priorities. You may say, "I already did that once." But now that you are pregnant, you have added a whole new twist to your life, turning your current list of priorities on its ear. It is time to step back and reassess those you keep and those you let go.

You will increase your peace of mind and reduce the mental stress of your pregnancy if you can get clear about what your priorities are and then act accordingly. Your clear priorities will:

➤ Help you to say no without guilt or angst.
➤ Give you added confidence and trust that you are making the right choices for yourself.
➤ Make your time as a pregnant woman a whole lot more fun and enjoyable.
➤ Keep you from looking back and having, or worrying about having, regrets.
➤ Allow you the time you need to think, rest, watch and listen.
➤ Stop the energy-draining internal agonizing.

Use this as an opportunity to freely throw all of the pieces of your life up into the air. Don't worry about what fits and what doesn't at this point, you'll get to that later. Begin this process by focusing on what matters most, what is the most fulfilling and what just sounds like a whole lot of fun. Then, with all the clarity of your top priorities and the motivation they contain, we will turn your attention to what it is time to leave behind. So get ready to leap into the opportunity of creating a fulfilling pregnant life for yourself.

Your First Pregnancy Priority

No matter what else is in your life, during pregnancy and on into parenthood, you and your baby must come first. You can give to others what you have remaining after attending to your baby and yourself. Another time in life it will be your turn to give, but right now, you are successful if you simply take good care of yourself and your baby. This is physically crucial and is one of the first skills you can build towards becoming a great parent. You, your partner and your baby need you to be your best possible self, and that can only happen with proactive self-care.

Pregnancy is a time for receiving. By receiving well, you will have so much more to give when the tables have turned and you find yourself on the giving side. How would life be different for you if you welcomed the giving of others? How can you enjoy this time of receiving? What would it be like to take the best possible care of yourself? What would that include? What would that exclude? Where can you begin making this shift in your life?

Clarifying the Rest of Your Priorities

So, now that you are pregnant, what matters most to you? Below are some exercises to aid you in setting your top ten pregnant priorities. There is no room for mediocrity. When you can only have ten, you need to get ruthless.

So get some paper and a pen. Label one page "My Top Ten Priorities" and use this special page as the place to collect your priority list. Write the numbers one through ten down the left side and then next to Priority One write "Care for myself;" and next to Priority Two write "Care for my baby." As we already discussed, these come first. Now you can have eight other  priorities in your life. Use these exercises to boldly clarify those most important aspects.

EXERCISE ONE: PAST PRIORITIES

You probably have some idea about what your priorities have been in the past. Maybe they were to get your college degree, buy a house, have exciting adventures with your friends or find a job you enjoy. These may have been written down as priorities or just interesting ideas that often popped into your head. Either way, a great way to get clear on where your priorities are now is to begin from a list of past priorities. From a list like this, you can see which priorities still play a key role in your life and which are no longer important to you.

Step One: Begin this process by writing down the first ten to fifteen priorities that come to your mind; that is likely enough to start with. These are the things, activities or people from your past that have had a lot of meaning and to which or to whom you have been very committed. If you are having trouble coming up with ten to fifteen, think back on where and how you have spent your time, money or personal energy. That is often a good sign of past priorities.

Step Two: Next, cross off all of the old priorities that are clearly no longer as meaningful or important to you.

Step Three: Finally, from those remaining priorities, circle any you know in your heart are still extremely important to you. One way to evaluate each is to ask yourself, "Would I want to spend my time on this if I knew I would be dying in the next six months?" A second way to evaluate the importance of a priority is to mentally send yourself into your old age and look back to the present from twenty or thirty years into the future. What priorities matter from that perspective? Use both of these methods to assist you in narrowing your list to those things that are the most important.

Congratulations, you have just identified several of your priorities. It can be just this easy. Write these priorities in your top ten list, filling priorities number three, four and so on.

Exercise Two: Turning Your Values into Priorities

Values often stay relatively stable through life, but major experiences, such as the one you are going through now can lead to some shifts or changes in your values. For some people, values can be one of the most powerful ways to uncover priorities.

Values are those ideals that you hold most closely to your heart. They often dictate how you respond to situations and what you see as positive or negative in your life. Knowing your values can significantly influence your priorities. To uncover some of your core values, begin by writing out a response to the following questions:

Describe a time when life was as perfect as it could be for you.

➤ What was important about that time?

➤ What was working in your life then?

➤ What was in your life then that is not in your life now?

If you took the time to find an answer to these three probing questions, you just uncovered three things that matter a lot to you. These are tied into your values and each is a possible priority in your life. Continue through the following three questions, answering each of their probes, and then you can look over all of your answers and see where your priorities stand.

Describe a time when you were the most miserable you can remember, when your life felt awful and you just wanted to give it all up.

➤ What made this such a terrible time in your life?

➤ What was missing from your life during this time?

➤ Where were you compromising on what mattered most
to you?

Your answers to these probing questions help you see what you cannot compromise on. They help you see some of the things you just cannot live with. From that kind of information, you can identify a personal value or current life priority. Notice what you found here and then move onto the next question.

Describe an occurrence that would be so wonderful it would seem like an impossible dream.

➤ What is almost too wonderful to imagine that it could ever
be a part of your life?

➤ What makes this such a wonderful prospect for you?

➤ What value does it hold for you?

Your answers here point to some of the important priorities that you may not be allowing yourself to pursue or that you may not be attending to as much as you should. Again, think about your answers to these probes and what they tell you about your values as well as your current priorities.

Describe a decision in your life that you agonized over, one that was difficult to make.

➤ What were you torn between?

➤ What did each these different choices represent to you?

➤ What did you value about each choice that made the
decision so hard to make?

➤ What was your reaction to the choice you finally made?

When you struggle with making a decision, it is often due to a conflict between your values; each possible choice you could make in the situation allows you to honor one of the values you hold close. So, in a sense, it often forces you to choose between two or more things that are very important to you. See what you can learn about your values in conflict with one another and what that can tell you about your current priorities.

Now look through all of your answers to these value-based questions and see what stands out as a priority in your now-pregnant life. What priorities do you want to add to your top ten list? On what values does it feel important to follow up? What values have been underrepresented in your life? Which values do you want more of in your pregnant life? Don't worry about the exact wording of a priority here, just get the concept of the value down. Some examples of concepts are freedom, family, accomplishment, time to yourself or room to be artistic. So, look through your own data and see what concepts stand out as important to you right now in your life.

For the purists, most would name this core value as the actual priority, this is the thing you want to pursue in your life right now. That is all well and good, but if your list had the word accomplishment on it, what does that tell you to actually do? How will you know what to do so that you feel like you are following through on your value of accomplishment?

To bridge this, I recommend pairing this value concept with a clear action that has meaning for you right now. For example, if your value concept was accomplishment, an example of turning that into an action would be writing a priority like this one: "Accomplishment — doing one thing a day to prepare myself for the arrival of our baby." If your concept was freedom, an example clarifying it with your specific action is this: "Freedom — brainstorm things I can do that allow me to feel free and then act on them so I feel like I still have my own personal freedom through pregnancy and into parenthood." Now you have a priority on which you can take direct action.

Write your value-based priorities on your top ten list. You may now be completing priorities five, six or seven. You will find that life is much better lived if your values show up in those things you make your priorities.

EXERCISE THREE: THE PREGNANCY WHEEL

Do you know what parts of the pregnancy experience are most important to you? If you are like most other pregnant women, you may be in touch with some more than others. Pregnancy is going to come and go very quickly, even though nine months can feel like a very long time when you are in it. Here is a chance to consider your pregnancy-related priorities. Use the Pregnancy Wheel to make sure you do not lose sight of those important parts of your pregnancy experience.

The Pregnancy Wheel on the next page is a tool for clarifying how satisfied you are with some of the significant parts of the pregnancy experience. Read through each of the headings, and if you feel a meaningful part of your pregnancy experience is missing from the wheel, add it by drawing a line from the center point out to the edge of the circle, dividing an existing wedge into two wedges and creating a new piece. Label this new piece with your additional pregnancy experience.

To explore your current level of satisfaction within your pregnancy experience, you will go around the wheel and consider your satisfaction with each wedge. Do this by imagining the inner tip of each wedge represents zero, meaning no satisfaction whatsoever with this part of your pregnancy experience; and the outer arch of the wedge represents ten, complete satisfaction with this part of your pregnancy experience. Go around the wheel and, for each piece, draw a line within the wedge somewhere between zero and ten, indicating your level of satisfaction, as has been done here in the sample wheel.

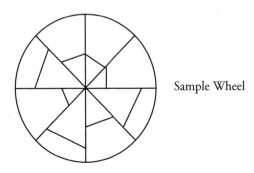

Sample Wheel

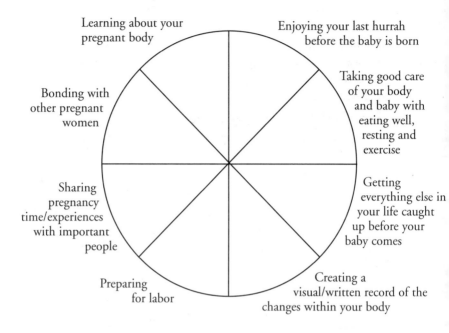

When you have identified your level of satisfaction with each wedge on the pregnancy wheel, look over the entire wheel and consider the following questions:

➤ What stands out about your wheel?

➤ What does your pregnancy wheel tell you about what you want?

➤ What is getting lost in the business of the day?

➤ Which of these pregnancy experiences do you want to make a priority in your life right now? There is no right priority here. You don't have to necessarily choose those you rated lowest. What is best is to choose those to which you know you want to give extra time and attention after going through this exercise.

Add these chosen pregnancy experiences to your priority list.

Your Top Ten Pregnancy Priorities

Now you should have a full list of pregnancy priorities. Look them over. Do they all fit for you? Is there any added fluff in the form of less important priorities you can cut out? Did you forget something that is critical to you? Some important aspects of your life that you may want to be sure you considered are:

> Your career
> Regular exercise
> Time with friends
> Quiet time alone
> Your partner
> Your extended family

Add, edit or delete what you need to so that you have the ten most important priorities on your list.

When you feel confident that you have compiled an accurate list of your key priorities, add any clarification you may need to be sure there is no doubt what each priority means to you and how you want to act on it. For example, on your first priority, care for yourself, what does that mean to you? Eating well, getting enough rest, exercising, finding time to read or limiting your activities each day. Everyone's idea of self-care is a little different, so get specific about how you will implement this priority.

Finally, for true clarity, prioritize your priorities. Overkill, you say? No way! Most coaches and life strategists would only allow you two to three priorities. With a full list of ten life priorities, you have more than you can put into most days. So, it is important you know what you want more of and what you can live with a bit less of. The value of allowing you these ten rather than the standard two to three is that for most people, the important aspects of life go far beyond what you can put into two or three priorities. The important people in your life can easily fill those three slots. Realistically, you need room for these important people, room for the important aspects of your pregnancy, as well as room for the interests and passions that bring fulfillment to your life.

To prioritize your priorities in an easy and useful manner, follow these two steps. First, with care for yourself and care for your baby as numbers one and two, rank your remaining priorities in importance from three to ten. Second, identify those priorities you want in your life on a daily, weekly and monthly basis. Now, at a glance you know what is most important to you and how you want each priority to show up in your life. All ten of these priorities are important to you; some are just getting more time and attention than others.

If this structure is getting to be too much for you, that is fine. Just take your priority list as far along this process as fits for you. We are all different and the goal is to provide an array of tools to assist you. Your job is to make the most of those that fit and leave behind those that don't.

As you move through your pregnancy, remember that things happen, changes occur, you will have new needs and wants. All of this can have an impact on your priorities. So, remain open to the fact that your priorities may do a little shifting throughout your pregnancy and still more shifting after your baby is born.

But for now and into your near future, you have a clear set of guidelines to help you plan your time and make your choices. There is no more agonizing about what you should or should not be doing — you know. Carrie was surprised by how much this kind of clarity helped her.

I had never been into all of that goal-setting stuff before. I knew what was important and just did what I needed to do when I needed to do it. But then when I became pregnant, I had a lot less energy and felt overwhelmed by my life a lot more quickly. I tried to just do less, but it never seemed to work out. Something important would always come up and fill any open space I had carved out for myself.

My husband is a big planner, and he was the one who helped me finally accept that I had to make some choices, set some clear priorities for myself and limit my commitments. It took some time, but I came up with a great list of what was absolutely most important to me. It was actually kind of fun taking the time to think about what I wanted most in life.

This list has been key in guiding what I choose to say yes or no to throughout my pregnancy. I feel confident that I am doing what truly matters to me. I posted my priorities next to my computer screen, and this has helped me stay on track with some of my self-motivated priorities, such as exercising or cleaning out the closet in the baby's room. Without my list, I know I wouldn't have been as good about fitting these into my life.

Where will your list of priorities help you? What have you learned about yourself by going through this process? How can you put this list to work for you? From this moment on, trust your priorities to help you make good choices, set limits, say no and ultimately take good care of your pregnant mind, body and soul.

From List to Life

The listing is over and now it is time to begin living your priorities and the resulting pregnant life you have designed for yourself. When it comes to following through and beginning to live your list, you are moving from a piece of paper buried on your desk to a concept that is alive and an integral part if your daily thoughts and actions. Here is a collection of options you can consider to bring your pregnancy priorities to life.

➢ Put your list of priorities in an obvious place and read them at least once per week. This could be in your calendar system, on your computer monitor, on the refrigerator or taped to your bathroom mirror.

➢ Read your list to your partner and ask for help in holding yourself accountable to these top ten priorities. Other options for building in accountability are to consider enlisting a friend or hiring a coach.

➢ Walk through the coming week or two in your calendar and ensure that it is filled with your priorities. See that the frequency of each priority fits with the daily, weekly and monthly guidelines you have set. If you find this is not the case, make some changes in your plans for the week or take a bit of time to re-evaluate the importance of that priority.

➢ Pick your top three priorities for each day or week and put them in an obvious place. Use this reminder to zoom in on a priority that can get lost in the business of a normal day.

➢ Stick a piece of masking tape to your body to remind you of a priority you are often forgetting. You could tape it to your hand, around a finger or inside your shirt. Everytime you see or feel it, you will be reminded of that priority.

➢ Set only realistic expectations of yourself and your actions when it comes to implementing your priorities. Don't erode your own peace of mind or waste your energy in mental thrashings due to a lack of perceived progress. Instead, remind yourself that you are doing the best you know how. When you know something will be particularly challenging, break it into a series of smaller manageable steps so each is no more than a comfortable stretch.

➤ Tell a group of people in your life about your priorities. You may want to go into detail on one that is particularly challenging on which to follow through. This will provide you with some helpful support or motivating peer pressure.

Which option will be the most helpful for you and your specific priorities? Choose one or two of the options that fit and then take the necessary steps to keep your new-found priorities alive.

Just Say No

To make any of this work, you must be able to say no to all of the other things that will siphon your energy away from your chosen priorities. Without "no," this small, yet powerful word, a clear set of priorities is not enough to keep you from running around responding to the constant requests made of you. Without the ability to say no, your priorities will quickly get lost.

We live in a world enamored with the "Just do it" tag line. However, an equally important balancer to this, whether you are pregnant or not, is the exact opposite: "Just don't do it." Making

priorities happen in your life requires that you do those things that are important to you and, at the same time, that you stop doing those things that are not important to you. The trick in living with both of these directives is in knowing which to apply where. Your priorities are just the answer you need. They give you a clear direction, and they motivate you to let go of those things that no longer fit. So, use your priorities to help you say no.

The first challenge to saying no is knowing what you want to say no to. Begin by checking in with your priorities. If it does not fall within the boundaries of one of your ten priorities, you probably need to say no. Some additional help in weeding out the no's can come from the following big-picture principles.

> If you are trying to convince yourself that it is something you should do, you probably shouldn't.

> If it takes more energy from you than it gives back, get rid of it.

> If it taxes you too much mentally, physically, emotionally or spiritually, no matter what it is, for the sake of your baby, stop!

> If it is alive and breathing and needs your help, you probably cannot say no to it. This is about helping those who need you such as a hungry dog, a thirsty plant, an injured child or a person in need. It is not about filling every request of a demanding neighbor, needy in-law or whiny sibling.

In addition, learn from those pregnant women who have gone before you and think seriously about saying no to things centered on alcohol — like happy hours or wine-tasting parties. What's the point? You cannot drink the wine, and even with the nicest people, it's boring to quietly listen to everybody talk about the various wines. You can also add to your list of things to avoid those dreaded movies and books involving horrific birth stories or aliens taking up residency in an unsuspecting host body. These can be a little too close to home.

Once you are clear on what you want or need to say no to, the second challenge comes in knowing what makes it hard for you to get that no out of your mouth. Look over some of the most common reasons people struggle with saying no, and see what rings true for you.

Everything seems so fun or interesting. Yes, our world is a virtual cornucopia of options. But too much fun becomes unfun very quickly, so just choose the most fun of the fun and enjoy that to its fullest.

You feel obligated to most everything and everyone. It is great to be helpful to others, but you were not born into this world to meet everyone else's needs. Your needs and wants matter, too. Stop serving others at the cost of yourself.

If you say no, you might miss some great opportunity. Life is a parade of great opportunities. Choose what fits you best, build satisfaction in the selections you have made and let go of the mental gymnastics over what other great opportunities you might be missing.

"Good" people don't say no. Think about these good people who never say no. Honestly, do you want to be living their lives? And what about all of the other good people out there who are saying no? Why not take one of them as a role model instead? Then you can be "good" and have a life that serves you, too.

No is not an option you were raised having. Old habits die hard, especially those that were wired in when you were just a babe. But with a bit of tenacity, you can let go of this and feel free to say yes or no as you choose. This may take some perseverance, reading some helpful resources, or meeting with a therapist or coach. Whatever it takes, break this chain so you don't pass the same condition onto your baby.

I just cannot get the word out of my mouth. If this is the case, practice. Say it right now. It doesn't matter who is sitting next to you. Let's hear it, a clean straight no ... good. Now think of some low-risk places where you could begin saying it: in restaurants, to telemarketers or door-to-door solicitors. For a while, say no at every low-risk opportunity you see. Then, begin to bring this word into some of the more significant areas of your life.

Saying no pits me against someone else. That is an interesting perspective. However, a more helpful truth to hold is that saying no is not against anyone but is instead for yourself. It is likely that your no will mean a lot more to you than it will ever mean to anyone else. The other person will probably have forgotten all about it by the time the conversation is over. And if someone you care about is offended or personally put out by your no, take some time to understand the reaction, express your own concerns and then find a way to ensure you both get what you need.

When you're pregnant, the process of saying no can be even more difficult. In addition to the constant challenge of declining, you also have to manage the added enticements of:

➤ Knowing this may be your last chance before the baby is born.

➤ Special attention because you are pregnant.

➤ Wanting more time with friends and family during this time.

➤ Wanting everything to be perfect for the baby's arrival.

➤ Wanting to live up to the social image of the perfect and together pregnant women.

All of these can pull at your heartstrings, eat your time and leave you running in circles. The reason you struggle with saying no has its own set of challenges to overcome, but by taking the time to understand your personal struggle and resulting challenges, you are well on your way to freeing yourself from its hold and creating the space to say no to options that do not fit.

You have begun to remove your personal block to the path of no-ness: you have mastered the first and most important step to saying no ... or no, thank you if you want to be polite about it. Some other polite and gentler options you may want to consider employing to skirt around the edges of no are:

➤ I don't think that will work for me.
➤ Not at this time, thank you.
➤ Could I get back to you on that?
➤ I'm just too busy right now. (This is probably true anyway.)
➤ It's just not the right time for me. (This can definitely be true when you are pregnant.)

If you need something softer than a crisp, clean no, find a phrase that fits your personality and still arms you with the power of no.

The final challenge with saying no is saying it to those specific people who make it harder than hard. You know who they are. Those people that can crumble your attempt with just a nod, a gesture or an inflection in their voice. These people are often:

➤ Members of your family
➤ Co-workers
➤ Certain friends
➤ Your partner

Add to this list, as needed, so that you have a solid handle on those in your life for whom an answer of no equates with a struggle. Then begin watching how you dance around your no's with these people. What do you put yourself through? What do you avoid? What burdens do you take on in the process? How do you let these people affect your ability to follow through on your own priorities?

Now think about saying no in the context of your priorities. How could you use your priorities to assist you in saying your no's to these people? Some options to consider are:

> Talking openly about your priorities and helping this person see that the request does not fit.

> Using another person as the excuse to meet an important priority. For example: my healthcare provider told me I needed to be getting to bed earlier, my partner is worried about me and would rather that I didn't do that, or, I just don't have a lot of free time because my mother wants to do a lot together right now.

> Telling them up front, long before a request is made that for a while you will not be very available as you focus your attention on your pregnancy.

Don't give your priorities and your power away to these people. Find the method you need to ensure you make the most of your short time as a pregnant woman.

Make a Commitment and Follow Through

In general, people who take the time to set priorities are often most thwarted by their own motivation to follow-through. To get what you ultimately want during your pregnancy, follow-through is as vital a step as setting those good, clear priorities in the first place. Without the follow-through, your priorities are just words on paper. You've got some priorities, but what are you doing with them?

Take a moment to think about what gets in the way of your ability to follow up on the things that are important to you now that you are pregnant.

> Is it a feeling? It could be one of not having enough time, being overwhelmed or being too tired at the end of a day. Ask yourself what part of this feeling is a perception of how life is or a true reality of the life you are facing. Then do what you must to change your perception as well as your reality.

> Is it a thought? It could be getting caught worrying about what pregnant women should not do. Maybe it's a concern that you will fail before you have even begun, seeing your priorities as basically unimportant or that they will just get in the way of other people's needs. Thoughts can rule our lives if we let them. So, take your power back and decide for yourself what you want, and then invite those destruc-

tive thoughts to jump off a cliff. They will likely attempt to climb right back up, so be persistent in moving them out.

➤ Are you bumping up against old habits you need to let go of and replace with new ones? Old habits can be challenging, but overcoming them just takes the simple act of doing whatever it is differently. Decide what you want to put in place of this old habit, and then go to it. The new habit will undo the old before your very eyes. Be aware that it usually takes two to three months of dedication to build a new habit that will last.

➤ Are you getting stuck in your own excuses, such as, I just wasn't born that way? Face the facts. You could do it if you wanted to, and for some reason you're just not doing it. But once your willpower is in place and you are ready to follow through on a priority, no excuse in the world will stand in your way. So, when you catch yourself making excuses, look for what is standing in the way of your willpower or thwarting your attempt to follow through.

➤ Are you just plain lazy and forgetful? Probably not. It is likely another easy excuse, a lack of motivation, a call for added support or a fear from which you are hiding. So, stop beating yourself up for your couch-potato tendencies and instead look at what is lurking underneath. Bring that to the surface, and you'll be back in action.

What is the unique challenge you face in putting your priorities into action? Take a couple of minutes to get a clear idea about your particular stumbling block. Then, if your pregnancy priorities are important to you, support your ability to say no, follow through and set yourself up for a life filled with all that matters most to you.

Summary

Sad But True, You Cannot Do it All

The Hard Decisions can be:
- Letting go of how things used to be.
- Saying no in difficult or challenging situations.
- Facing the challenge of foregoing the "I'm important" high that comes with living a very busy life.
- Stretching as you begin to act on the choices you have made for yourself.
- Making yourself do what you committed to, even when you don't feel like it in the immediate moment.

The Resulting Peace can be:
- Finding you are your own best keeper.
- Freedom from the nagging guilt of all those "should haves."
- Freedom to choose without the added weight of regrets.
- Finding the time you need for what is most important in your life.
- Tapping into a renewed sense of personal energy.
- An alignment with all that is most important to you.
- Clarity about your own power to do whatever you decide for yourself.

Resources

On Setting Priorities

Living Your Best Life: Work, Home, Balance, Destiny: Ten Strategies for Getting from Where You Are to Where You're Meant to Be, Laura Berman Fortgang. (New York, NY: JP Tarcher, 2001.)

Falling Awake: Creating the Life of Your Dreams, Dave Ellis. (Breakthrough Enterprises, 2001.)

Time Management from the Inside Out: The Foolproof System for Taking Control of Your Schedule and Your Life, Julie Morgenstern. (New York, NY: Henry Holt, 2000.)

The Procrastinator's Handbook: Mastering the Art of Doing It Now, Rita Emmett. (New York, NY: Walker and Company, 2000.)

Take Yourself to the Top of Your Life: How the Secrets of a Leading Life Coach will Help You Achieve Success, Laura Berman Fortgang. (Thorsons Publisher, 1999.)

Take Time for Your Life: A Personal Coach's Seven-Step Program for Creating the Life You Want, Cheryl Richardson. (New York, NY: Broadway Books, 1999.)

First Things First Every Day, Stephen R. Covey, A. Roger Merrill and Rebecca R. Merrill. (New York, NY: Fireside Books, 1997.)

First Things First: To Live, to Love, to Learn, to Leave a Legacy, Stephen R. Covey, A. Roger Merrill and Rebecca R. Merrill. (New York, NY: Fireside Books, 1996.)

Life Launch: A Passionate Guide to the Rest of Your Life, Frederic Hudson and Pamela McLean. (Santa Barbara, CA: The Hudson Institute Press, 1995.)

The 7 Habits of Highly Effective People, Stephen R. Covey, A. Roger Merrill and Rebecca R. Merrill. (New York, NY: Fireside Books, 1990.)

Strategy Four
Ease Your Way into Parenthood During Your Nine Months of Pregnancy

From the moment you find out you are pregnant and begin planning for that day when you bring your baby home, you are on the road to parenthood. It begins in many small ways, but ultimately ends up meandering its way into every square inch of your being. No matter what else happens in your life, from this point on, at some level, you are always a parent. It is one of those few and far between life experiences that leaves you forever changed.

Parenting while you are pregnant is similar to life as a newly hatched bird. You have some initial time to dry off your feathers and get to know the ins and outs of operating your parenting wings. Then, in one dramatic push, your baby is born, you fall from the nest, instinct takes over, and you soar into parenthood. Now, while you are still contained within the safety of the nest, you have an opportunity to make some choices, set some plans and begin to build your parental peace of mind to ensure your initial flight into parenthood is as smooth as it can possibly be.

Choosing for Two

In pregnancy, you start becoming a parent when you realize the hit-you-upside-the-head fact that you are no longer choosing just for yourself, you are also choosing on behalf of your baby. At first it is just here and there, but, as time passes, you begin to see your parental urges influencing every choice you make, from the very small, such as what you choose to eat or drink that day to the very big, such as whether or not to keep your job. Cindy and her partner caught a hold of this change when they where about halfway through their pregnancy.

All of a sudden, as if a switch has been flipped, I see both my husband and myself realizing it is time to make choices and life decisions which take into account the arrival of our coming baby. Well of course, you say, my baby will be here in four months. But oddly enough it has not been that obvious to either of us.

I was actually quite shocked the first time I found myself having to choose between my own needs and the needs of this baby inside of me. It happened about a month ago. I was jazzed about signing up for this six-month intensive learning opportunity. It included three, five-day retreat experiences; one of which I would have to do after the baby was born. "Okay," I thought to myself, "I can do this. My husband can help. Maybe he can bring the baby to the last retreat and take care of it so I can nurse it during those five days." I came home and asked him what he thought, and it was clear he thought I was nuts. We talked about it and decided that I shouldn't do it. But I still wanted to. I continued to strategize ways I could make it happen.

As the days progressed, I saw that I was trying to squeeze too much into a small space. Once I realized this I knew it was time to step back from the normal pace of my work life. It was time to make some different kinds of decisions. I felt an acceptance and new peace of mind about the baby-oriented direction my life was taking. I had made the choice to make this child a priority, and it felt as if I were stepping into parenthood with both feet. My right answer was to take the focus of my energy off activities related to furthering my career and instead turn my focus toward building this new family.

Ironically enough, a week later I watched my husband go through a similar shift. He wrestled with the idea of building a spec house during the time of our pregnancy and the early months of our child's life. This was all going to happen on top of his regular, full-time job. After much soul searching, he came back and told me he wanted to keep his focus on this pregnancy, our new baby and adjusting to becoming a dad. This building project would not allow him the opportunity to do any of that. He also realized it was time to focus on parenthood.

We are both making major life choices with our unborn child's needs in mind. This is something totally new and feels like the beginning of parenthood. I know there will be things that are important to me that I won't choose to put aside for my baby. But those choices will be carefully evaluated. The bottom line is clear. I will be living my life differently than I did prior to the birth of this child.

Becoming a parent does not mean you need to sacrifice what is important to you. Instead, it is about making good choices to ensure you are there for your baby and you have what is most important for yourself. These choices can oftentimes be very challenging; usually, you are trying to decide between two or more things that matter to you. When you are facing those agonizing parental choices, it can be very helpful if you:

➤ Look at the decision from both the short-term and long-term vantagepoints, two years out vs. ten years out. This exercise gives your decision added depth and increases the quality of the choices made. What aspects of the decision change as you move from a short-term perspective to a long-term perspective? What do these different perspectives tell you about what matters most to you?

➤ Get creative and see if there are ways you can turn the tables slightly to have more of or maybe even everything you want.

➤ Remember that one of the biggest reasons people struggle with making good choices is because they get their priorities mixed up. So look back over your priorities and remind yourself what is most important.

➤ Eliminate the fallacy that one choice is going to be right and the other somehow wrong. See all of the options as potential "right" answers for yourself and, instead, just decide which of the right answers you most want to choose.

➤ Look for any "shoulds" you carry around that may be clouding your ability to make a good decision. These are unhelpful mental rules such as "I should earn my share of the family income" or "I should love the idea of staying home with my child." Listen for these "shoulds" when you talk about your tough decision; chances are you will hear yourself actually saying, "I should blah blah blah." Once you have uncovered your own shoulds, move them as far from your decision-making process as possible. Make your parenting choices based upon what is best for you and your unborn baby, free from the entanglements of an assumed should.

With all the noise of our culture, and boy, it's loud, finding your own best parenting answers is, without a doubt, challenging. As you begin moving into your role as parent, the goal is to get good at listening to what is most important for you and your child. The suggestions listed above are ways of clearing away some of this June-Cleaver-clutter on one side and the life-in-the-fast-lane-hype on the other so you can hear your own true voice.

An Initial Balance Between Work and Family

While you are still pregnant, the task of designing an initial plan for balancing your work, personal needs and demands of your new family can be your biggest parenting task. Maintaining a balance between work and family, as well as taking care of yourself in the process, is often one of the larger, ongoing challenges of parenthood. Chances are your life is already overflowing and you know that to fit in the demands of parenthood, some things will have to change. Maneuvering through this highly charged evolution will pull on every priority you have and send your values locking horns with one another. Wendy and her partner ran headfirst into this quagmire.

I think I would name week sixteen of this pregnancy Rubber Meets the Road. My husband and I are talking about what life will be like once this baby is born and, unfortunately, we have found that our ideas look quite different. What we have been talking about is how we will manage our new life with a baby when I go back to work.

All along, my plan has been to go back to work on a part-time basis, ten to twenty hours a week. To this we are in agreement. Where we differ is about the care for our child during those hours. My husband wants to get daycare to cover these work hours and have me work a fixed set of hours each week. I, however, feel strongly that we should use daycare as little as possible. His job has very unusual working hours, why can't he be in charge of the baby for twenty hours each week while I am at work? Let's take advantage of this flexibility. I can schedule my work around his. He was not happy about this idea at all.

We both have strong feelings, our ideas on how to set this up are so different, and we can't go and each do it our own way. We have to find an alternative we can both agree on and live with. On top of all that, caring for our unborn child is such a loaded issue to begin with — well, the you-know-what hit the fan. We had a real wing-digger. Finally, after the dust settled a bit, we realized that I was afraid he would not commit to parenting responsibilities, and he was afraid that I would not do a good job of scheduling my work time and contributing to our family's income.

We uncovered the true issues — what mattered to each of us. Now, we could stop talking about daycare and focus on these two issues. We could express our concerns and help one another understand what mattered. We don't have this situation solved yet. It will take time, some experimenting once the baby has arrived, and listening to each other. But at least we now know we can support one another through the process and trust that we will devise a solution that works well for all of us.

It is not easy to make these kinds of decisions with so much unknown; a new baby, a new work schedule, maybe letting go of a comfortable job. It is tough to find a solution that feels best for your baby, yourself and your family as a whole. If you have spent any significant time building your career, how do you choose to let it go or take time away from it? This career can feel like your first baby. Will you be able to walk back in where you left off once your tenure at home with babies is over? Be with your baby, keep your own independence and earning power, be fulfilled and satisfied, how do you put it all together? No wonder the thought of life after your maternity leave is headspinning.

One of the best ways to get the most of what you want is to break the traditional mommy mold and get creative. Don't do it like anybody else. Let go of your all-or-nothing thinking and see what interesting options you can come up with. When doing this:

➤ Take some time to consider the potentially meaningful parts of your family and parenting responsibilities, as well as those most important parts of your career. Then look for ways to keep yourself connected to each and get some help with handling the others. For example, if evenings with your baby seems important, begin considering how you can return to work and keep evenings at home as sacred time with the family. Or, if a specific aspect of your current work is your favorite, look for ways to keep that and let go of some other less desirable part of your job.

➤ Don't assume anything is out of the realm of possibility until you have asked and gotten a firm no. There are so many ways to put things all together. If you see an option you are interested in, don't shoot it down before you've tried. Pursue it.

➤ Recommit to those parts of your life that you have identified as your priorities and design your initial work and family balance to ensure these priorities can show up in your actions.

➤ Remember that what is important to you also counts, it is not all just about the baby's needs or your partner's needs. It is critical to keep your personal needs in the picture. If too much goes unmet, it will come back around and your baby will be one of the ones who catches the brunt of your dissatisfaction, so pay attention.

➤ Don't stop tweaking the plan until it fits ... again ... and again ... and again. You know how life is, just when you think you've got it all down, you are thrown a new curve ball. These unexpected zingers seem to come even faster when delivered from your baby, so keep an eye open for the next required alteration.

Make an agreement with your partner to strategize until you find a balance with which everyone is comfortable. Life is too short and babies grow up too fast to spend years unsatisfied or unfulfilled.

WORK AND FAMILY CHOICES, CHOICES, CHOICES

If you find that looking at your options leaves you frozen in indecision, feeling like you have no options, or just the opposite, completely overwhelmed by options, you can count yourself as very normal. Many people respond by avoiding the choice and just drift through the decision. Drifting is always one option, but it does leave you open to chance and the randomness of life. Choosing, by its nature, asks you to look at what you want and set a direction. It takes a bit more work on the front end, but pays off on the back end.

You can choose to design your life as a parent in an infinite number of ways. And, along the way, you can change that design an infinite number of times. Throughout the years, there could be work, school, volunteer activities, part-time jobs, full-time jobs or a combination of any of these all at one time. What matters most in designing a parenting life strategy is that you like the life you have designed. If you do not, it is time to design a new one. All of these various parenting lives have their unique ups and downs. Let's play around with the pros and cons of four different choices you could make.

Mixed Choice Number One: Parenting with a Full-Time Job. Maybe you are leaning towards parenting your newborn baby with the added demands of a full-time job. How do you perform a full-time job around the added full-time responsibility of being a parent?

The Ups: It is likely that you can continue furthering your career without risking any of the professional or financial setbacks that can come with taking time out to raise a family. You will get time every day to be free of baby spit-up, your teeth will most likely be brushed each morning and you will still be able to enjoy the luxury of calm moments with something warm to drink.

And the Downs: First of all, know that no matter what you are doing in your job, you will never stop being a parent. Your heart will remain connected to your baby, no matter where you are physically located and this reality can be painful when you are away. You will often feel this gnawing loss that you are missing out on something very important; hours to just sit and hold your baby in your arms, those wonderful little baby smiles, or all of the firsts that will be viewed by your baby's caregiver. You will likely feel stressed and torn between your baby's needs and your work responsibilities and every time you leave your baby crying at the daycare provider because you're running late, your heart will break. You will give it everything you have, and it still won't be done.

Put all of this together, and you have one good option to consider.

Mixed Choice Number Two: Parenting with a Part-Time

Role. Maybe you are leaning towards parenting your new baby with the slightly less demanding responsibility of a part-time position, going back to school or committing to a significant volunteer responsibility.

The Ups: This choice allows you to keep your foot in your career and still be there for a significant amount of baby time. You get to have some sane time to be an adult with other adults without it taking too much of a toll on your physical, mental or emotional sanity. In some great ways, this option lets you have all of what is important to you.

And the Downs: The price for all of this personal fulfillment is scheduling stress, little personal time and the constant mental juggling that comes with simultaneously balancing two significant life roles. Taking time to spend those meaningful hours with your baby, as well as get your work commitments met, is like squeezing juice from an onion, and at the end of the day you are completely empty. You will have little or no extra anything in your life, but it will be the richest and fullest time you can ever imagine.

If you are cutting your hours in a job you have been working at full-time, realize that a common down of this can be feeling like you are now out of the loop, limited to working on less exciting projects or having to give up a significant portion of your leadership or more intriguing responsibilities. If you will be working fewer than thirty hours per week, most organizations don't see you as being at the job enough hours to keep a handle on these larger aspects of your job. You've done more and you know you can do more, so working this watered-down role can be a struggle at times.

Put this all together, and you have a second good option to consider.

Mixed Choice Number Three: Parenting without an Outside Job. Maybe you think you want to stop working altogether in any kind of a paid position and stay home full-time with your newborn baby.

The Ups: Ah, the charm of this simplified option. You get to focus all of your attention on caring for your baby and building a wonderful home for this child. You'll have the opportunity to have fun adventures together and none of the stress of long work hours away from your baby, due dates or maneuvering around meeting schedules. You have the time to create some very thoughtful traditions for you and your family, and you have the energy to keep strong connections with extended family and friends. You will have the luxury of taking the time away from your baby as rejuvenating personal time, during which you can do nice things just for yourself or those you love.

And the Downs: Until POP — the bubble bursts — and you realize you forgot to set up any time for yourself, you realize you don't actually like staying home all of the time or you begin to lose your sense of confidence. You can forget who you are as a separate person from the baby. You can go batty spending so much time on your own with your child. You can feel ignored or undervalued in a society focused on careers and accomplishments. Or, you can find your self feeling trapped by this child and this lifestyle.

Put this all together, and you have a third good option to consider.

Mixed Choice Number Four: For Those Who Want to Stay Home with Baby But Need to Have a Job. Many of you may feel that financial need has already made this decision, and you cannot even consider another choice. This situation can leave you feeling like the only side you have is down. You are facing a financial reality, but before you give up on your option to stay home with your newborn baby, be sure you have looked good and hard at what you define as financial necessity.

The Truth: What could you live without? Really, other than your love, time and attention what will your baby need? Don't let our consumption-oriented society limit your choices. I cannot say it loud enough — take the time now. Decide what you want and consciously choose. Any answer is great as long as it fits with your values, who you are, what you want, and what is best for you and your family. So, if what you want is to stay home with your newborn baby, work to find a way that you can have that and still pay all of your bills. Some ways you can do this are to:

➤ Stay home, care for your own child and, in addition, provide in-home daycare to other working parents' children.

➤ Find a position that allows you to work from home. It

needs to be something you could do on your own time,
when the baby is sleeping or happily occupying herself.
These kinds of positions could be word processing on your
home computer, telephone work or writing projects. Begin
your search for this kind of a position in the resource list at
the end of this chapter, in your local classifieds or by calling
a larger temporary employment agency.

➤ Start your own home-based small business. Find something
you are excited about and see what you can make happen.
Keep it as limited as you need to, to fit it into the hours
you have available. Two successful examples of this are a
mother of two boys who painted decorative floor mats and
a stay-at-home dad of a young daughter who sold sports
paraphernalia for his alma mater. One caution here is that
small businesses can take some time to turn a profit, so be
prudent if you need this income to meet your basic living
expenses. See the reference section at the end of this
chapter for ideas on getting started in this direction.

➤ Look into a living situation where you could be a caretaker.
You would have work to do, but for the most part you
could do it with your baby along.

➤ See if there is an older person who needs some in-home
care and would enjoy the company of you and your child.
You could be paid for this option or possibly create some
kind of a live-in arrangement depending on the circumstances. There are older people with very large homes, and
this could be a win-win situation for everybody.

➤ Look at purchasing a duplex. Then you could use the rent
income to offset your reduction in pay from your job. All
of the work associated with caring for and renting the
property could be done with your baby in tow.

➤ Provide pet-care services to those going out of town or
working long hours. You and your baby can have lovely
walks each day with a collection of thankful animals.

➤ See if there is a relative or colleague with which you would
be interested in sharing your home. The rent money they
paid would again offset any reduction in your income. If
you are seriously considering any of these living arrangement options, be very careful that you are honest with
yourself about whom you feel good sharing living space

with and whom you do not. Inviting someone you are not comfortable with into your home will only create another problem you don't want to have to think about when you arrive home with your new baby.

On the flipside, if you feel best having some part of your life or your work that is still yours — claim it with pride. Find a position that fits and pays enough to afford good daycare for your child.

Put this all together, and you have a fourth good option to consider.

All four choices have their own sets of mixed blessings and none is a complete walk in the park. They all have their moments where the highs are breathtaking and others where the lows stink. Great parents can be found making each choice. Don't let anyone or anything pressure you to do something that goes against your natural grain. Take the time to understand what matters to you and choose the experience that fits this time in your life. By next year, it may all be different and you will get to go through the process of choosing again. Change comes often in a parent's life.

BALANCING LIFE WITH YOUR NEWBORN BABY

No matter what life you choose for yourself, you can count on the fact that you will face the challenge of keeping it in balance once your baby is born. Here are some hints to help you out. Some things you can do to keep life in balance if your intention is to work outside the home while parenting are to:

> Set up special play dates with your baby wherein you have some uninterrupted time together. This is not time when you make dinner, clean up or anything else other than enjoying one another. You roll around on the floor together or look at a book, go for a walk or make funny faces at each other. You and your baby can do all of the other chores of life together after you have had some time to play.

Don't give this time away for anything; your baby is growing up so fast and chores are neverending.

➤ Call your baby's daycare provider once every day to check in and see how she is doing.

➤ Limit your overtime at work. Set up this boundary and hold to it with zealous determination.

➤ Do whatever you can to avoid overnight travel as a part of your job. If you do have to travel, come up with creative ways to bring your baby along. Maybe you have Grandma come to care for the baby while you are working, or you cut out any of the extras and get the trip down to one or two days at most.

➤ If nursing your baby is your choice, make the effort to continue nursing though you're at work, even if it is challenging, to maintain all of the benefits of this powerful connection. For so many reasons, it is worth the added complications.

➤ When you leave your baby to go to work, catch yourself if your day is spent pining for your baby. If you have chosen to be away from your baby to work, make this the best work you have ever done. Don't be away from your baby to waste the time wishing you were with your baby. When you're with your baby, be with your baby, and when you are at your job, be at your job. If you don't, you end up unfulfilled most of the time and, with that kind of result, what's the point? You want to be able to leave your job and all of its worries behind and come back to your baby refreshed and ready to focus all of your energy on parenting.

➤ Get ruthless about knowing your priorities and saying no. This may be a no to work, a no to a family project or a no to that friend who wants to get together for a play date. Be thoughtful about your limitations, know them like the back of your hand and then follow through with your actions.

➤ Every once in awhile, find some time that is just for you. This may be getting your hair cut, or spending an hour frivolously shopping or having a massage. It doesn't matter what it is, just that you are doing something that gives new energy back to you. Some of you may find you need to do this more often to keep yourself feeling balanced and others of you may need this less often. Either way, find your own rhythm and then respect it.

➤ Finally, read through the list below for stay-at-home parents and take what is useful to you.

Some things you can do to keep life in balance if your intention is to stay at home and parent full-time are to:

➤ Do whatever preplanning or preparation you personally need to maintain your peace of mind during your day with your baby. This could mean preparing for your day the night before, planning one fun activity each day, getting any loose ends tied up or finding activities that will meet your needs, as well as those of the baby. Achieving this calm state will allow you to be more present to your baby and yourself and to fully enjoy this time with no regrets or misgivings.

➤ Sit down and intentionally plan how you want to ease out and, later back into your career or work life. The plan for coming back in may have to be altered as you change over time, but it is invaluable to have a working plan. Doing so will help you remember that in the big scheme of things, you have other parts of your life which are separate from your baby. On those bad parenting days, this clarity can be a life-saver.

➤ Determine the professional contacts you would like to maintain while you are away from your job. Then, make an effort to stay in touch through phone calls, emails, lunches, letters or some form of a fun monthly mailing.

➤ When you or your partner feel a pang of regret at the news of a nonparenting colleague outclimbing you on the ladder of success, step back and honestly assess if your priorities have changed. If not, reaffirm yourself to the choices you have made and the priorities you are holding. If your priorities have changed, make some new decisions to get yourself back into the game.

➤ Consider using this time away with your baby to make a career or work change, letting go of a past role and beginning to think about what you want to pursue when your baby goes off to school or whenever you decide to add an outside job back into your life. Commit to take several hours every month to explore your postbaby future. Use this time to consider work options that give back to you mentally, spiritually, physically and/or emotionally.

➤ Finally, reread the above list for working parents and take from that what will also be helpful to you.

No matter what career/family life you decide to pursue, create an initial plan and then give yourself a wide opening to change your mind. It is very common for your plan to change and evolve as you begin caring for your baby. Don't lock yourself into any one option now or even three years from now. As you and your baby change, so too will your preferred life balance. Through all of this, remember that you have choices, even if it seems like you do not ... the real truth is that you still do.

To Daycare or Not to Daycare — That Is the Question

If you determine that you need childcare, finding a situation you feel good about can be a tough process. Who is safe for your baby? Will they love her? How will you protect your baby there? Where is Mary Poppins when you really need her? It can be grueling to figure out what you want and then challenging to find it. And as painful as that first visit can be, you can find a place where you feel good leaving your precious baby.

There are many ways to set up childcare for your baby. Listed below are a few of the more common options along with a pro and con unique to each. Look them over and see toward which you naturally gravitate.

Daycare centers
Pro: Facilities are governed by strict state guidelines.
Con: Baby is exposed to more illnesses of other children.

In-home daycare
Pro: A more intimate environment is provided.
Con: All of your trust is resting on one person acting responsibly with your baby.

Nanny
Pro: Your child can stay in your own home.
Con: There is nobody watching to ensure the nanny is always doing the right thing for your child.

Nanny shared with one other family
Pro: Your child has the advantages of a nanny with the added bonus of a playmate.
Con: You must coordinate your schedule with that of another family.

A relative
Pro: They have the potential to give the most loving care your child could possibly receive.
Con: They may be very vocal about their opinions of your child and how you are raising her.

Childcare co-op with another parent
Pro: The cost of your childcare would be your own time.
Con: You would have to care for someone else's child to cover every hour that you had your own child watched.

This list is in no way exhaustive, but it gives you a good place to start. As you go through your search for good childcare, you will create a full pros and cons list based upon the specifics of your unique situation.

Now, take your initial preferences and combine them with a clearer understanding of what you want from a childcare provider. Use the questions listed below to help you gain this understanding.

➤ When it comes to childcare, what is best for you?
➤ What is best for your partner?
➤ What seems best for your unborn baby?
➤ Whom do you want acting as the primary caregiver for your child?
➤ How much childcare do you want?
➤ What hours would you need covered?
➤ What criteria are important to you if you looked at a daycare away from your own home? (Examples: clean facilities, warm and loving staff, modern equipment, for-profit or nonprofit, diversity of other children, location, policies on sick children, infant-to-caregiver ratio and flexibility in meeting the unique needs of your baby)
➤ What criteria are important for you from a caregiver in your own home? (Examples: trustworthy, reliable, good references, age or gender of the provider, that she will

follow your directions and your sense that she enjoys
your baby)

Let your answers to these questions guide you in clarifying what
you want. Don't let anyone else's ideas of the right answer to this
one get in the way of identifying what is best for you.

Once you have the field narrowed down and you are ready to
begin meeting some providers, you can find them by:
> Calling friends in your area who have children in daycare
and asking them for referrals or how they found a provider.
> Looking in the Yellow Pages.
> Contacting the city offices to see if they keep a listing of
daycare providers.
> Contacting your local school to see if they can connect you
to a list of daycare providers.

As you make these connections, don't be shy. Work the contacts
you do find to get the most you can from them. Ask for referrals,
lists of daycare providers, how you can go about finding a provider,
how others have found a provider and if there is anyone else they
know to whom you can talk. Don't hang up until you have an
answer that satisfies you to each of these questions.

When you have a list of potential childcare providers, do a little
bit of sleuthing to check on their reputations. Check to see if your
state has a childcare resource and referral service, or call the
National Child Care Association; contact information is listed in
the reference pages at the end of this chapter. Speak with these
organizations about your center and see if they have been reported
for any child injuries. Call the provider and have an initial conversation, identify some important questions you can ask all of the
providers you are considering and ask for a few references. Then call
all of those references and see what their experience has been. It is
your child's life you are looking out for here, so don't be sloppy on
this one.

Once you have found some providers you are interested in
visiting or meeting, go see them with your partner. This will make
it easier for the two of you to make the decision together. Gather
information on the procedures they have for storing breast milk if
you're nursing, cleaning the infant area, eating solids, child devel-

opment, discipline, sleeping, staff screening, as well as any other criteria that is important to you. When you visit, keep your eyes open for the following:

> What is your gut reaction telling you? Pay attention when your intuition tells you that this is not the way you want your baby cared for. It doesn't have to be rationally explained, just move on until you find a provider with whom you are comfortable.

> Can they care for your baby if he or she has any special needs such as autism, Down's syndrome or physical limitations?

> How do you feel in their presence or facility?

Finding good childcare will be key to maintaining peace of mind when you are away from your baby.

Baby-Induced Fiscal Responsibility

An additional place where you as a parent are choosing for two during pregnancy is in your finances. On the road to parenthood, many people go through something similar to a religious conversion to suddenly decide to get financially responsible. A well-tended financial life seems to become an important part of creating a secure place for the baby. This could be looked at as an extension of that nesting process everyone talks about. Sue's experience highlights just such a conversion.

My pregnancy was a surprise. We had been trying to get pregnant for years with no success. I had missed my period for four months and thought I was going into menopause only to find out I was pregnant. So, I made my transition into parenthood on a fast track. When I found out I was pregnant, what I wanted settled most of all was our finances. I wanted to be sure everything was balanced and up to date. I denounced all of my bad financial habits. I wanted to make sure my baby was coming into a financially secure situation. If that were in order, I knew we could provide a safe and stable home.

Financial messiness can drain your peace of mind and eat up precious energy you will want to spend caring for your baby. If you feel the need to get responsible financially before your baby is born, trust the importance of this feeling and commit to doing the following:

> ➤ Set up a payment plan you can stick to and begin the process of ridding yourself of credit card debt.
> ➤ Make an appointment with your partner to seriously sit down and create a family budget that includes all of the needs of your coming baby. Adding a baby to your life has all kinds of financial implications. They include increasing your living expenses, potentially decreasing your work time and thus your income, saving for college, and preparing for your child's finances if you and/or your partner were to die. Give these issues the thoughtful consideration they require.
> ➤ Look at the challenges you face in maintaining financial responsibility. This could be an over-the-top interest in shopping, sloppy record keeping, decadent habits you cannot afford or the lack of a consistent income. Address your personal issue head on now, while you still have some free energy. Make it your goal to have this challenge contained before the baby is born.

Financial responsibility is not hard. It is one of those things that looks a lot tougher than it is. All it takes is a bit of knowledge, a few decisions and some discipline. Use the resources listed at the end of this chapter to help you get started.

Parenting's Most Perplexing Paradoxes

When it is all said and done, one of the trickiest aspects of parenthood is the ability to traverse an array of perplexing paradoxes. You are constantly asked to do one thing for your baby and oh, by the way, do the direct opposite as well. Thankfully, they come on gently as your new baby grows over the months. But if you look closely, you can already see the buds of these paradoxes taking shape in your life. By the time your cuddly baby is a raring-to-go toddler, you will be stumbling upon the riddles contained within these paradoxes on a daily basis.

Some of the paradoxes of parenting come and go as your baby grows and changes. Others, however, remain ever-present throughout the duration of your parenting tenure. Strengthen your parenting muscles by gaining some comfort with these paradoxes now. Here are four paradoxes that can challenge you in some way during every single year of your child's life.

PARENTING PARADOX ONE: BE CONSISTENT AND MAKE EXCEPTIONS

Babies like structure and, at the same time, life is full of so many exceptions, requiring flexibility from all of us. Consistency helps your baby learn about how life works and what to expect. It allows your baby to begin to trust that her needs will be met and that she is truly safe. Exceptions allow for spontaneity and adventure, they teach your baby about celebrations and taking part in the wonder of the present. What a gift to begin life with the ability to maneuver between both sides of this paradox.

Where is your personal challenge in balancing consistency and exception? Are you currently able to integrate consistency and exception within your life? On which side do you tend to err? How do you respond when you notice yourself getting uncomfortable with one or the other? Do you find yourself cringing at the thought of having anything consistent or structured in your life? Do rules rule in most of what you do?

Assistance if you are challenged by the looming call for consistency: For your newborn baby, the consistency side of this paradox shows up around feedings and sleeping, basically the two activities that fill a newborn's world. This does not mean that you need to be home every day by 12:30 so your baby can nap in her crib and that your feedings must be every two hours on the dot. Either is a fine example of creating consistency for your baby, but there are also unlimited other options for creating consistency. Anything will do as long as it creates some kind of a routine that your baby can come to expect. It is unpredictable randomness that is a setup for confusion and frustration for your baby and, as a result, for you. If it is hard to consider creating and then sticking to a routine structure:

> ➤ Find a unique routine you can stomach and then stick with it as long as it continues to meet the needs of you and your child. Remember that any routine is okay, as long as it is a routine with which you and the baby are comfortable. For example, Jan's son Alex had the unlikely routine of napping in the car each day. She would consistently arrange her

schedule so they were in the car around the time that Alex was getting tired. An unusual routine, but one that worked for both of them. Look at creatively designing your routines so they serve without locking you in.

➤ Think ahead so that wherever you are, you are prepared to follow through on a consistency in your baby's life. This could mean bringing things for the baby as well as yourself, planning errands or events around the normal routine, or just taking a break in the action to tend to your baby's routine.

Assistance if you feel the hairs bristle on the back of your neck at the thought of making exceptions to your consistent routines: So the flipside of this paradox is about making exceptions. Exceptions require you to notice those times when it is important to do things differently than you normally would. If you are challenged by the thought of making room for exceptions:

➤ Create a structure for yourself around making exceptions. Set a goal, starting today, to make one exception to a normal structure every week. This will allow you to begin practicing, so by the time your baby arrives, you will have built up your tolerance for exceptions.

➤ Find some people in your life that are good at making exceptions to their consistent routines and watch how they do it. If you can, ask them about how they go about making exceptions. What do they notice about making exceptions? What works for them? What do you see them doing?

As a parent to your beautiful baby, find a happy medium between building some supportive routines and, at the same time, watch for the opportunity exceptions provide to wander outside of the regular lines of life.

PARENTING PARADOX TWO: SET LIMITS AND CREATE SPACE TO EXPLORE

Your baby is dependent upon you to ensure her world is safe and, at the same time, that she is stimulated and exposed to all that will benefit her mental, physical and emotional growth. Limits will help your baby learn to keep herself safe and maintain necessary boundaries. Creating room to explore will bring zest and adventure to her life. By successfully combining both sides of this paradox into your parenting, you will help your child learn to know and maintain her own healthy limits, as well as develop an ability to venture bravely into the world. What a powerful foundation from which to begin building a life.

And where is the challenge for you in balancing this paradox of life with limits and wide open spaces? Are you living with a set of limits held so closely that it insulates you from exploring and experiencing all that life has to offer? If so, continuing on can lead you

to build the same for your baby. Or, just the opposite, these tightly held limits could send your grown baby out into the world seeking the constant rush of life without limits and the adrenaline high that goes with it. Maybe your struggle is around living a life with too much space, lacking in a healthy set of limits. Which direction do you need to lean to balance this paradox within the context of your parenting?

Assistance if you see yourself wimping out when it comes to setting limits: From birth to college you will be called to consistently set and hold limits for your child. If setting limits is your challenge, try the following.

➤ Remind yourself that when babies cry due to limits their parents have imposed, they are expressing their discontent, not a feeling of abandonment, mortal fright or a broken heart. They still love their parents, and they still know their parents love them. They just don't like the ramifications of the limit that was set. It can help to identify some related words to your baby's frustrated cries, something like, "Hey, Mom, Dad. I don't like this," "Hey guys, I want to be with you," "I want that toy, I liked that one!" These requests are much easier to say no to than "Waaaah! I am totally abandoned and broken, please save me!"

➤ Begin by setting a limit in just one area, choose something that is easier for you to follow through on or a limit that will have a big positive effect on you and your family.

Remember that your child is looking to find the edges around acceptable behavior, and your limits will help her get clear much faster. She actually wants you to provide some guidance in the form of limits.

Assistance if you are overwhelmed by chaos at the thought of providing space to explore: This is the time when your baby is wandering outside of the edges of your limits. If it looks to be hard for you to create the space for your baby to explore and appropriately adventure into the world or beyond your limits, try the following.

➤ Take some time to understand what your concerns around exploration are. Are you afraid your child will get sick, choke, or fall and get hurt? Or, maybe it is more psychologically oriented, the fear that, with exploration, your baby will venture out into the world too quickly. Once you know what your fear is, then you can make some logical choices to ensure there is safe exploration in your baby's world without a fear controlling your decisions in this area.

➤ Talk with other parents about how they saw their babies beginning to push on limits and explore. Find out what they did to encourage the adventurous spirit of their children.

Babies are fragile and need to be kept safe. At the same time, like us, they are more robust than we give them credit for and hunger to explore all that is new.

PARENTING PARADOX THREE: TEACH A LOT AND LEARN EVEN MORE

As a parent, you are asked to be both teacher and learner. Your baby is designed to learn from you. She is constantly watching you to decipher how it all works here in her new world. Your child is continuously adapting to all you present. And at the same time, your baby comes with so much to teach. She is telling you what she needs, she is teaching you about how to be her best parent, and she is expanding your personal insights and awareness every day you are together.

How do you see yourself wearing the simultaneous hats of teacher and student? Is it challenging to step into these opposite orientations? Where do you see yourself having the confidence and patience from which to teach? Are you someone who likes to know, to have all of the answers? Do you know how to find your way into the stance of a student and listen to the teachings of another? Even from one so much smaller than yourself?

Assistance if the thought of teaching leaves you with a case of stage fright: In parenting your baby, the teaching you will do is basically about ... well ... everything. You will show her how to love, trust and connect to others. You will teach her about communication, beauty, music, humor and patience. You will help your child understand her own body, how to eat, when to sleep and the joy of play. If it is overwhelming for you to step into the role of teacher-of-all-things, try these suggestions.

> ➤ Remember that you are the perfect person for the job. You have everything your baby needs. The focus is not on you doing it all perfectly but instead on your baby having what she needs to continue developing. You will have the opportunity to teach throughout every minute of every day. So, if you mistakenly let an opportunity go by, don't worry, just raise your awareness to catch the next one coming your way.

> ➤ Pause and take the time necessary to teach. Sure, it would be faster just to do it yourself, but the whole point here is not efficiency; instead, it is about helping your baby learn, gain her own insights and grow up.

Assistance if you fear you have forgotten how to be a learner: At the same time your small, yet-unborn baby will provide you with the opportunity to learn more than you ever imagined about ... well ... everything. You can expect your baby to open you to learning about love, patience and fulfillment. She will teach you to get creative, to improvise and to be resourceful beyond your wildest dreams. She will teach you about flexibility, your connection to the world and a deeper sense of spirituality. If you see yourself challenged by the thought of learning from your baby try the following.

> ➤ Shift your opinion of your child from helpless newborn to a complex and wise creature who has just arrived here, still aware of what was left behind.

> ➤ Take some time to consider the distinct advantage your child has over you. She is, as yet, uncluttered with social

noise and comes to everything with a clean outlook devoid of the judgements or hang-ups that can hamper the rest of us.

➤ Learn from the information your baby gives you. Look at her physical reactions, listen for a change in her cry or notice when her eyes sparkle.

➤ Try just asking your baby a question, something like: "What can I learn here?" or "What do you need?" Then give yourself some downtime for the answer to surface. You may be surprised to find that listening from the perspective of your baby will lead you to a much better solution than you could come up with by yourself. Begin practicing this while you are still pregnant and see what happens.

Wisdom comes in many forms; right now, it just happens to be in a very small and sometimes quiet bundle, so listen closely.

Juggling the Teacher and Student Roles Together as You Parent: When you step into the roles of teacher and student simultaneously, you can bring the wisdom and richness of both perspectives to your baby. As a student following the leads of your baby, you are looking to your baby for information and guidance. What does she need from you? What does she teach you about living life? With that data, you are aggressively leading the way to create an environment that will support the needs of your baby and enrich your own life.

Instead of running off in your own direction as a parent to your baby, your parenting is attuned with and in service to your baby. You are still the caretaker and responsible party, but the focus of your parenting is on serving the needs of your baby. You are serving when you stop and pay attention to who this child is rather than placing her in your box of life labeled "baby." She is not fulfilling a generic script in your life, she is her own entity, living out her own uniqueness. See these unique qualities in her and let your understanding of them lead you to be the best possible parent for her.

PARENTING PARADOX FOUR: LOVE AT UNFATHOMABLE DEPTHS AND LET HER GO

One of the most wonderful gifts of parenthood is that it can bring with it an effervescent sense of joy and powerful feelings of love. Never before could you have imagined such an intensity of love filling your life. At the same time, your job is to help this person, the new source of love and fulfillment in your life, to grow up and ultimately away into her own life.

Even before this baby has left the womb, some experience the parenting reality that this child is going to continually grow farther and farther away. And as painful as it feels, achieving this is actually a gift to your child and considered successful parenting. Ouch! How do you let go of someone you love so much? This letting go can be one of the biggest agonies of parenting, and it begins sooner than you would ever expect.

For most new parents, the challenge in this paradox is in the letting go. But for some, the intensity of this love can be the truly scary part. It is one of the most intimate relationships you can have. What will it be like for you to love this child? Which of your own limitations will challenge you in this kind of a relationship? And how will you respond when you first see yourself being asked to let go and make space for this child to move into the world? Will it be during her first week of life when you realize that this beautiful little baby will grow up faster than you can fathom, or will it will hit you the first time you leave the baby in the care of another?

Assistance if you are afraid of so much love: You are probably already feeling some love for your unborn baby, but if the thought of this relationship filled with the deepest of love appears overwhelming, consider these suggestions.

> ➤ Remind yourself of the fact that this little baby is the safest possible person to love in this way. She thinks you are the most beautiful, wisest and most inspiring person ever. There are no judgements attached to your baby's love. When she is older, it may feel altogether different, but for now in her eyes you are the top of the top.
> ➤ Talk with your partner about your concerns. Think about what support you would like to help you in adjusting to the power and intimacy of the parenting experience.

Assistance if you realize it will be hard to release your ironclad grip from your baby: With the love quickly comes the letting go. You don't need to look too far ahead to find your baby beginning to grow up and away. If letting go of your baby is your stumbling block in this parenting paradox, try these options.

➤ Read the children's book, *I'll Love You For Always,* or one with a similar message of letting go, over and over until you can get through it without shedding a tear. Sounds kind of odd, but it will help you release some of the emotion and get you more comfortable with the part of letting go that is the natural order of things. Letting go comes from finding comfort in the different seasons of life. Hold on because in parenthood spring, summer, fall and winter all begin moving at supersonic speeds.

➤ Look at your challenges in letting go and find out what is hard. It could be the insecurity of loss, the fear of losing someone you love, the pain of change or the obvious passage of time. Then attend to the specific piece that is the most painful for you.

Your baby desperately needs your deepest love and, at the same time, to be released to go out and live a full and healthy life of her own. Parenting from a balanced perspective around this paradox will be one of the greatest gifts you can ever give to your baby.

Summary

The Early Signs of Parenthood

The Thrills that Await You :

➤ Developing new skills or habits that will help you care for your baby.

➤ Beginning to feel a spark of the most incredible and fulfilling love you quickly develop for your baby.

➤ Getting to know a whole new part of your partner.

➤ Finding life filled with more sense of purpose than you ever imagined.

➤ Realizing how much parental wisdom you already have and how much more you have to gain.

The Pains of Your Transition:

➤ Struggling with a clash of priorities.

➤ Finding yourself uncomfortable with some of the new demands you're placing on yourself.

➤ Finding yourself uncomfortable with the responsibility of this new parenting role.

➤ Realizing the details of parenting are another topic you can add to the list of things on which you and your partner disagree.

➤ Realizing you must give up some parts of your current life to make room for your new baby.

Resources

On Parenting

New Parent Power!, John K. Rosemond. (Kansas City, MO: Andrews McMeel Publishing, 2001.)

The 7 Worst Things (Good) ParentsDo, John C. Friel, Ph.D. and Linda D. Fried, M.A. (Deerfield Beach, FL: Health Communications, Inc., 1999.)

Whole Child / Whole Parent, Polly Berrien Berends. (New York, NY: HarperPerennial, 1975, 1983, 1987 and 1997.)

Becoming the Parent You Want to Be, Laura Davis and Janis Keyser. (New York, NY: Broadway Books, 1997.)

Smart Parenting, Dr. Peter Favaro. (Chicago, IL: Contemporary Books, Inc., 1995.)

On Mothering

The Spirit of Pregnancy: An Interactive Anthology for Your Journey to Motherhood, Bonnie Goldberg. (New York, NY: McGraw Hill.)

The Mother Trip: Hip Mama's Guide to Staying Sane in the Chaos of Motherhood, Ariel Gore. (Seattle, WA: Seal Press, 2000.)

Mothers Who Think: Tales of Real-Life Parenthood, Camille Peri, Kate Moses and Anne Lamott. (Washington Square Press, 2000.)

The Mother Dance, Harriet Lerner. (New York, NY: HarperPerennial Library, 1999.)

The Birth of a Mother: How the Motherhood Experience Changes You Forever, Daniel N. Stern, Nadia Bruschweiler-Stern and Alison Freeland. (New York, NY: Basic Books, 1999.)

The Hip Mama Survival Guide: Advice from the Trenches on Pregnancy, Childbirth, Cool Names, Clueless Doctors, Potty Training and Toddler Avengers, Ariel Gore. (New York, NY: Hyperion, 1998.)

Laughter and Tears: The Emotional Life of New Mothers, Elizabeth Bing, Elizabeth D. Bing and Libby Colman. (Owlet, 1997.)

A Mother is Born, Merete Leonhardt-Lupa. (Bergin and Garvey, 1995.)

Recreating Motherhood, Barbara Katz Rothman (New York, NY: W. W. Norton Company, Inc., 1989.)

Mother Journeys, Maureen T. Reddy, Martha Roth and Amy Sheldon (Minneapolis, MN: Spinsters Ink, 1994.)

Mothering, www.mothering.com
A magazine and online website focused on issues of mothering and natural family living.

On Fathering

Fathering Right from the Start: Straight Talk About Pregnancy, Birth and Beyond, Jack Heinowitz and Wade Horn. (Navato, CA: New World Press, 2001.)

Great Dads, Jonathan P. Decker (Holbrook, MA: Adams Media Corporation, 2000.)

My Boys Can Swim!: The Official Guy's Guide to Pregnancy, Ian Davis. (Rocklin, CA: Prima Publishing, 1999.)

The New Father Book: What Every Man Needs to Know to Be a Good Dad, Wade F. Horn, Alice Feinstein and Jeffery Rosenberg. (Better Homes and Garden Books, 1998.)

Fathering: Strengthening Connection With Your Children No Matter Where You Are, Will Glennon. (Berkeley, CA: Conari Press, 1995.)

The Expectant Father: Facts, Tips and Advice for Dads-To-Be, Armin A Brott and Jennifer Ash. (New York, NY: Abberville Press, 1995.)

101 Ways to Be a Special Dad, Vicki Lansky. (New York, NY: McGraw Hill, 1995.)

BabyCenter.com, www.babycenter.com/dads
A hangout just for men.

On Child Care

Expanding the Family: Need Childcare Answers?, Childcare Resource & Referral Network. (Minnesota Department of Human Services and the Minnesota Childcare Resources and Referral Network, 1993.) To order booklet phone: (612) 721-0265.

Childcare Aware Hotline
Phone: (800) 424-2246
This organization can give you the phone number for a childcare referral agency in your location.

www.nccanet.org
National Childcare Association. Address: 1016 Rosser St., Conyers, GA 30012. Phone (800) 543-7161.

On Home-Based Businesses

Home-Based Business for Dummies, Paul Edwards, Sarah Edwards and Peter Economy. (Hungry Minds, Inc., 2000.)

Working from Home: Everything You Need to Know About Living and Working Under the Same Roof, Paul Edwards and Sarah Edwards. (New York, NY: JP Tarcher, 1999.)

Making a Living Without a Job: Winning Ways for Creating Work That You Love, Barbara J. Winter. (New York, NY: Bantam Doubleday Dell Publishing Group, 1993.)

On Financial Savvy

Smart Couples Finish Rich: 9 Steps to Creating a Rich Future for You and Your Partner, David Bach. (New York, NY: Broadway Books, 2001.)

The Road to Wealth: A Comprehensive Guide to Your Money — Everything You Need to Know in Good and Bad Times, Suze Orman. (Riverhead Books, 2001.)

9 Steps to Financial Freedom: Practical and Spiritual Steps So You Can Stop Worrying, Suze Orman. (Three Rivers Press, 2000.)

Strategy Five
Call Upon Your Internal Strengths when Facing a Situation You Cannot Control

Welcome to the less-than-fun awakening: You are not the complete master of your own destiny. We tend to live life as if we we're running the show of our own life, and then something comes along to remind us that we are not as in control of it all as we once thought we were. Or, just the opposite, we are so overwhelmed by what is in front of us that we feel totally out of control, when in fact things are basically being handled. Whichever challenge you face, struggling with a time of life that feels out of control can push all of your buttons and leave you worn down, stressed to a nubbin, and having to learn a huge lesson in the power of surrender and letting go.

Believe it or not, finding peace of mind in all of this requires more letting go than controlling. The good news is that this lack of control does not need to result in wild screaming or gnashing of teeth. There are steps you can take to reconnect with your internal power and find some personal control in situations that are seemingly out of control.

The first thing to do is stop feeding the mushroom cloud of panic that is forming over your head and realize there are still things within your sphere of control. The following are the big and small choices you can make for yourself each day:

➤ Your mental attitude
➤ What you choose to put into your body
➤ How much rest you choose to get
➤ Your preparation and initial plans for labor and birth
➤ Asking for a second opinion when faced with a critical issue

➤ Your ability to get additional information on a desired topic

Taking action in the areas you can control will take some of the sting out of the areas you cannot control.

The next step is to rebalance your expectations of control in pregnancy. Unfortunately for those who really crave control, pregnancy is a place where you don't have as much as you may be used to. In pregnancy, you have the ability to make good choices but little authority or influence over the pending outcome. The up side is that most of the time everything works out just fine. But pregnancy is one of those rubber-meets-the-road life experiences that brings you face to face with the reality that faith, hope and trust are as important as planning, preparing and accomplishing. Even when you do all of the right things, the well-being of your baby as well as yourself is ultimately out of your hands. The truth of this last statement can be one of the biggest points of angst for many pregnant women.

The third step is to invest some time and energy into getting more comfortable using three internal strengths we all have available to support us through the worst of what an out-of-control pregnancy moment can send your way. These are:

➤ Simplify the drama of your perceptions

➤ Find a comforting hold when facing the unknown

➤ Rebalance your mental seesaw of fears and worries

The bulk of this chapter will equip you to apply each of these internal strengths to the realities of your unique pregnancy.

As your pregnancy leads you bellyfirst into a host of situations that push upon your desire for more control, it is bound to affect you in different ways. Don't be surprised if you find yourself reading this chapter again. Control, like peace of mind, is not something we can ever lock in; it is constantly ebbing and flowing in and out of our reach. Like so much in life, finding comfort with the coming and going of personal control is a balance of letting go and holding on. Take what you find to be the most useful for you in these pages and commit to do something with it. Do it as a gift for yourself.

Your First Place of Strength:
Simplify the Drama of Your Perceptions

For most of us, one of the biggest contributors to seeing life as out of control is based on our feelings and perceptions of a situation, how reality appears to be in the moment. Your perception is tied to how you feel, it can impact all other parts of your life in a very dramatic way, and it can swing to far-reaching extremes in the span of a day or sometimes an hour. Perceiving a situation as out of control is all it takes to have you responding like a chicken with its head cut off. We have all been there at some point in our lives, when you feel totally overwhelmed by something only to discover it wasn't so bad after all. The challenge is all in the perception you hold on the situation.

Some of what makes this normal experience of feeling out of control more intense during pregnancy is that there is so much happening in a short period of time. The whole pregnancy experience is incredibly new and emotionally loaded. The result is that instead of occasionally perceiving your life as out of control, you feel this way at some level every week or even every day. This can get uncomfortable pretty quickly.

Terry was no stranger to feeling a loss of control during her first pregnancy, but the true power of her perception hit her right between the eyes when she met with her midwife after having her water break at thirty-six weeks.

I was in a meeting when I began to feel water seeping between my legs. I left the meeting and went straight to the office of my healthcare provider only to find that my water had broken and I was going to have the baby right then. I was shocked and freaked out and overwhelmed. Most of all, I was not ready to have this baby!

I burst into tears. I still had so much more to do before this baby came. I hadn't practiced enough for labor. The baby's room wasn't painted yet, and we still didn't have a mattress for the crib. I had three projects at work that had not been handed off to a co-worker, and to top it all off, my mother was supposed to be here to help me with the baby when I came home from the hospital.

All of this came tumbling out to my midwife. She patiently listened, sat down next to me and said, "Yes, this is unexpected, but let's take one thing at a time and talk through the alternatives and choices you have." We walked through each of my concerns. She helped me to realize that the baby didn't care about its room or its crib; I had some great friends who could help get whatever needed 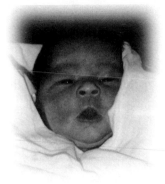 *to be ready while I was in the hospital. I had selected skilled people to take over these three important work projects and they would likely step up to the plate and ensure nothing fell through the cracks. She reassured me that I was having a baby and not going to the moon — my work colleagues could still call me if they needed anything from me. She said that maybe I would actually benefit by having my mother here to help me four weeks from now.*

It made such a difference to see all of these things from a new perspective and have someone help me solve those problems. I headed over to the hospital calm and ready to focus my attention on labor, delivery and my new baby.

Taking Back the Reins of Your Perceptions

So you have this ingrained set of buttons that, when pushed, sends your perception of control off the deep end. It is a normal human response. However, when that overwhelming feeling of losing control strikes, you don't have to remain caught in its grip. You will definitely feel its discomfort, but there are ways to contain it and give yourself some peace of mind.

As uncomfortable as it may seem, your perception is actually in your control much more than you may realize. This can be a bummer to face up to. Sometimes, in the heat of it, melting down just feels a whole lot easier. But, once that release of emotion is over, all it really takes to find some solid ground is to reframe how you see the situation, much like the midwife did for Terry. She helped Terry see her concerns and overwhelmed feelings from a different perspective. Doing this on your own will not always be easy, but here are some options you can consider to keep your perceptions serving you, as opposed to the other way around.

Catch It Early. Be alert to the early warning signs of feeling out of control. These are things like a feeling of becoming overwhelmed by small things, irritability, stress, increased emotions, overeating or the inability to sleep. Get to know what out of control looks like for you. For example, if you find you get hyper or crabby, use this reaction as a flag that it is time to refelct and discern what is growing out of your perception versus truly based in reality. An accurate assessment here will keep you from climbing a mountain when all you are really facing is a molehill.

Identify Specific Concerns. Move from a general out-of-control feeling to pinpointing specifics. For example, if the overall experience of coming home from the hospital with your new baby feels out of control, make a list of your specific concerns around this event; maybe it is how you will sleep that night or what you will do with yourself the first hour you are home. When you have a general out-of-control feeling, you can get a handle on it by breaking it down to specifics, what parts you are reacting to. Now you can begin to make some tentative plans about how to manage each of these specific concerns. This strategy gets you out of your cloud of confusion and allows you to pinpoint the one or two things of most concern. With this kind of clarity, you now have something you can work with.

Identify Some Positive Actions. When you are really clear about what feels out of control, identify a couple of positive actions you could take to minimize or even eliminate the stress you feel. Think about what you want, what would be most calming to you or what speaks directly to your concern. The most effective way of doing this is to begin by choosing something small. Oftentimes, getting started is half the battle, and once you take some positive action in that out-of-control area, no matter how small, the whole situation begins to feel better. For example, when you notice you are feeling anxious about the well-being of this baby growing inside you, you could call a friend, call the nurse, lie down and rest for a while, write a letter to your baby, eat a healthy snack or read one of your baby books. By choosing a positive action, you are providing yourself with some alternatives to pursue besides sitting and stewing in your out-of-control juices. You are reframing your experience. Taking action can allow you to see a more balanced picture of your current situation, and the result will be a reduction in your perception of life as out of control.

Exercise. Given the current state of your body, the last thing you may want to do is think about exercising, but pushing yourself beyond this initial wall of resistance will provide you with access to a whole host of benefits. Exercise signals your body to produce endorphins, which, when released into your system, provide you with added energy, a sense of well-being or peace, and often an improved outlook on life. By making this choice to exercise, you are giving your body an opportunity to take advantage of these endorphins, burn off some of the stress that can come with feeling out of control, as well as build up strength to support you through the pregnancy and labor. Choose something that is relaxing and pleasurable for you, like taking a walk, swimming or stretching.

Organize One Other Part of Your Life. Why not do the dishes or straighten up your desk? This sounds kind of crazy, but it works. Feeling like things are in control in one area of your life, no matter how insignificant, will positively impact your perception of how you feel about all of the other parts of your life. So, even though your kitchen has nothing to do with your pregnancy, giving it a thorough cleaning can leave you feeling like you have a handle on life and are ready to deal with whatever comes up next in any arena, including your pregnancy.

Provide Yourself with Some Form of Structure. Situations seem out of control when your mind whirls around and around with all of the different parts of the situation dancing in and out, stumbling on top of each other. Creating a structure to house those thoughts allows you to contain them in one place — usually a piece of paper — and keeps them from ricocheting back and forth inside your head. For example, if you are inundated with concerns about the care that your first child will receive while you are in the hospital delivering your second child, commit some time to writing down these concerns and then organizing a list of desires or instructions for each concern. By putting some structure in place for yourself, you take away a lot of the mystery surrounding the situation and will feel some relief by knowing you have done your best to get the situation into as much control as possible. Some possible structures to consider are lists, mind maps or creating a table.

Whether real or not, your perception has validity just because it is yours. You can help yourself respond to and work with your own perceptions by respecting your reactions and then taking some action to keep a balanced and comfortable mental state. What do you need to do right now to manage your perception of a situation with which you are currently struggling?

Turning a Difference of Perception into a Strength

Because your perception of control is just that, *your perception,* you and your partner may have very different reactions to a situation: while one of you may be struggling with a situation that seems totally out of control and overwhelming, the other may simply see it as a normal part of the process and consider it nothing to get too alarmed over. David has a great example of this:

When we were pregnant with our second child, I became very focused on the house. I felt like my ability to control the maintenance of our home was going to slip away as soon as the second baby arrived. I was convinced we would have little or no time to do anything with two small children to take care of, that this was my last glimmer of opportunity to get anything done and I had to take action. So I decided that anything I ever wanted finished had to be completed before the baby arrived. This had me on a home-improvement frenzy. My wife was not as concerned but went along with me.

Then, one day, she declared a stop. "I've had it," she said. "We have done enough to the house. It is time to stop." She felt like I was not attending to the reality of our coming baby and preparing to support her during labor. That was a wake-up call for me. In my fear of losing control around the house, I had gone a bit overboard.

When you perceive a situation differently from your partner, the way the two of you will both gain some internal strength is to acknowledge and support one another in these differences. Each of you sees it in your own way, and it can be very hard to nail down whose reality is actually the "right" one. Some specific actions you can take to strengthen yourself as well as your partner are to:

➤ Talk about the different ways you're seeing the situation and the concerns you have or the areas that feel out of control.

➤ Make room for the other person's perception of the situation to be valid. There are many "accurate" perceptions for every situation we face; maybe the one your partner is holding is just one that is hard for you to see.

➤ Encourage each other to take some action or give time to the out-of-control area, even if it is not something you see as a problem.

➤ Find ways that you can get or give support around the part of the issue that feels out of control.

Part of supporting and strengthening one another through your pregnancy is being able to understand what triggers each other's out-of-control feelings. What do you want to tell your partner about your current perception of being in control? What are the similarities and differences in your perceptions?

Your Second Place of Strength: Find a Comforting Hold When Facing the Unknown

In pregnancy, it is not just your perception that can lead you to feel out of control, there is also the basic reality that pregnancy is an experience filled with unknowns over which you basically do not have any control.

Science is wonderful at shedding light into many of these dark unknown corners of pregnancy. At the same time, especially for a first-time pregnant woman, there is just a lot that is new and unknown. For many of us, living with this kind of unknowing is uncomfortable.

THE INSTABILITY OF NOT KNOWING

What does living with the unknown feel like for you? What impact does it have on your day-to-day life? Jill gets to some of the uncertainty of it all when she describes the unknowns she sees in her up coming labor process.

I feel like labor will be one of the biggest experiences in my life—all of the pain, the emotion and the intensity. From here, I feel like I can't even fathom what I am getting myself into. I have this image of labor as being tethered to a pillar in the middle of a hurricane. There will be times that are just fine and there will be times that are intense and scary. This sounds like kind of a negative image, yet it doesn't feel negative to me, just overwhelming. And in the midst of all of this, whatever happens, I just have to keep on coping with it. I have a friend who just delivered her baby by scheduled C-section and, in a way, that would remove so much of my concern. I could plan for it, know when it was going to happen, and know what to expect from it. I guess the bottom line is that I don't have any control over what is going to happen, and that is such a challenging place to be.

Karlie, who is expecting her second child, has identified the blind trust that is often a part of living with the unknown when she says:

I have no idea how I will care for this baby along with my two-year-old. Many people have more than one child, and they all seem to survive, so clearly it is possible. The simple logistics of it all seem mind-boggling. So I am trusting that it will work out... but from where I stand now, I just cannot see how.

There are so many different kinds of unknowns. You may wonder about:

> Your pregnancy and how the shifts and alterations in your daily life will materialize in the next nine months
> Your labor and what that experience will be like
> The physical form of the baby and if it will be properly formed and healthy
> Your medical staff — how competent are they? Do you trust that they are paying attention?
> Others' reaction and how those you care about will respond to you and the decisions you make throughout this pregnancy process
> Your baby as a new member of your family — who the baby will be, and how will you react to her

And it's not as if you get to calmly address each of these issues one at a time. Instead, concerns about each of them tend to rise and fall continually throughout the pregnancy. For many people, living with this amount of the unknown at one time can really pull the plug on their general sense of personal control. To top it off, how all this is resolved is often less about you and what you do and more about all kinds of factors that are out of your sphere of control.

On the flipside, the unknown of your pregnancy is what makes the whole experience so intriguing and exciting. What will it be like to spend those first days in the hospital with your baby? Who will the baby look like? How will you feel about nursing your child? None of this can be known, and all of it is an open opportunity for excitement and anticipation. How beautiful it could be. Create an ideal picture for yourself of what the unknown could look like without setting your expectations of reality here — because, who knows — it is, after all, still unknown. As much as you can, enjoy your pregnancy experience to its fullest and trust the peace of mind you build even without having all of the answers.

Six Anchors to Secure Your Hold

While you are busy trying to steady yourself on this sea of the unknown, you have some internal guides positioned to keep you from drifting too far off course. Think of these as your anchors: They are your deeply held beliefs or personal truths, and although some of them may be a bit rusty or buried under a pile of seaweed, they are still tied with a reliable knot and can safely moor you in the rough waters of the unknown.

So where do you find an anchor that is right for you, your own unshakable truth that can aid you in becoming more comfortable living with not knowing? Some places to look are in your:

- Optimistic attitude or general orientation towards life. Such an anchor could be: "The world has an abundance to offer that I can use to support me in successfully traversing this challenge."
- Perception of how things are and the truths you tell yourself. For example, a useful truth could be: "I have built a strong support system, and it will shelter and support me as I need it to."
- Connection to something spiritual or larger than yourself, such as affirming: "I have a creator who cares about me and will help me in any challenge I face."
- Successful navigation of a past challenge of any size. An example of this could be: "I have faced big challenges before, and I can do it again."
- Anger, frustration, fear or sadness. Strong emotions are often a guide to something that is really important.

Therefore, pay attention to them. They may clue you into something that will be useful to you. It could be helpful to remind yourself of something like: "I know that my emotions are a gift, turning my attention to look in a new direction."

➤ Ability to see things from a big-picture perspective, using a statement like: "Soon I will know. Until then I focus my intensity on caring for my unborn baby with dedication and wisdom."

Each of these anchors provides you with a steady truth you can hold onto and at the same time allows you to gain some peace of mind by releasing the stress that comes with not knowing. The best thing is to find a truth that fits and has personal meaning for you. There is no easy, follow-the-steps answer to finding these anchors, but trust that you are your own best expert. You may want to try out a couple of different anchors. What are the anchors, core beliefs or personal truths on which you have successfully relied in the past? The best way to keep your balance in the choppy seas of the unknown is to trust your own instinct. Once you have found an anchor that really fits for you — use it!

Your Third Place of Strength: Rebalance Your Mental Seesaw of Fears and Worries

For us human beings, there seems to be a corollary relationship between losing our sense of control and the mounting of our fears and worries. There are a million different ways that fears and worries can sneak into our unsuspecting psyche and snatch our piece of mind right out from under us. And although they all have the ability to present themselves as giant monsters, by facing them head on, they can easily be deflated to the size of a rubber ducky floating in your bath — present, attracting attention, but easily maneuvered.

Each fear or worry that you hold says something a little different about you and the concerns you are facing. Three very common fears or worries that can emerge out of all the changes accompanying pregnancy are concerns about yourself, concerns about your baby, and those uninvited nightmares (or daymares) about both you and the baby. Here are three women's experiences with these common pregnancy fears and worries. Each woman is pregnant with her first child, and they are all at different places in their pregnancies. As you read each person's story, look inside yourself and see what you need to take away to build your peace of mind amidst your own fears and worries.

SOMETHING IS WRONG WITH ME!

Margo identified fears for her own health and safety as common throughout her pregnancy. She had several fears that were constantly residing in the back of her brain, but this one hit her like a ton of bricks.

It was very early in the morning. I was just waking up, and as my hand passed over my stomach, I was shocked to find a funny hard lump there. My heart began to race — oh my God, my mind screamed — I have cancer!

I began violently shaking my husband. "Wake up," I strained, "Wake up. I've just found a tumor in my abdomen."

My husband was groggy, "What? What are you talking about?" he said, running his hands through his hair.

"I have a tumor in my abdomen. It could be cancer! Oh, why now?"

"Wait, wait, let's just calm down for a moment. Why do you think you have cancer?"

"This lump in my abdomen. I never noticed it before. It is so hard and round."

My husband took my hand in his, "Honey," he said calmly, "you are pregnant."

"But it is off to the side here. It's not in the middle of my belly where a baby should be." I began to cry, big heaving sobs. What would I do if I had to choose between the life of my baby and my own life?

"Sweetie, there is a lot moving around in there, it's probably just your body adjusting to the baby." My husband put his arms around me and just held me while I cried.

Maybe he was right. I suppose a lot could be shifting around in there. Maybe the baby has pushed my kidney or bladder out of the way and it was causing this hard lump on my side. I'd never felt anything like this before in my own body. I had felt something like it in someone else's body — my dad's — and it was cancer. I began sobbing again.

"That lump could be our baby all balled up on one side, maybe your uterus shifts around as you sleep. I don't think you have cancer. This is probably just the beginning of you physically noticing that you are pregnant."

His comments made sense. "You're probably right," I said as I wiped my face with my fourth tissue. We lay back down, and I began showing him where the lump was. Craddled in his arms, we talked there for an hour. We were laughing about the whole thing by the time we sat down to breakfast. As crazy as it sounds, it felt so very real and incredibly scary at the time. There is just so much about my body that is changing — it leaves me feeling lost about what is normal and what is not.

Margo's husband was right. The lump in her abdomen was their growing baby boy, but at the time, the fear for her own safety was truly overwhelming. It's not crazy to have such fears. It doesn't happen very often in the Western world, but women do still suffer life-threatening complications bearing their children. If you are finding you have a lot of fears for your own well-being during pregnancy:

> Talk with your healthcare provider about scheduling additional appointments to discuss your specific concerns and check the changes in your body.
> Talk with your pregnancy partner about your concerns.
> Avoid all books, movies or TV shows that focus on a mother dying, especially in childbirth.

Keeping your focus on what is going right and asking for some additional support are critical first steps in calming your fears and worries for your own safety.

It may also be helpful to look at what happens to trigger these fears or worries and how your response may be helping or hindering you in getting through the fear. You may find there are specific people, like those who are full of tragic stories, or specific situations, such as those where you were hurt once before, that now increase your fears for your own safety. Take note of these trends and protect yourself from them by staying away. In addition, your own response to a fear or worry can cause you added unrest. You may mentally turn a fear into reality or a worry into truth. If that is the case, catch yourself when you begin to feel overwhelmed by a fear or worry and bring things back into alignment with reality. Step back from what feels like truth and identify what you currently know to be true.

SOMETHING IS WRONG WITH THE BABY!

Dawn talked about how quickly her ability to trust that her baby was okay could evaporate. She remembered one time when this fear took over and, in minutes, she was convinced her baby had died:

I was in my eighteenth week, and I had spent the evening with a co-worker talking about miscarriages, of all things. I left feeling the realities of how fragile a pregnancy really is. The next morning, I began feeling nervous as soon as I woke up. I followed the same routine that I had for the last several weeks, I lay very still in bed with my hands resting very lightly on my stomach, hoping to feel the baby's movement. And, just like every other time, I felt nothing. This, combined with my lack of a bulging stomach began to get me worried. What was going on in there? In addition, I'd been experiencing some strange sensations, like a muscle spasm around my cervix and abdominal pains, which, after calling an experienced mom, I decided were normal. But then, when I got dressed that morning and I could cinch my belt two notches tighter than I had been able to the day before, I lost it!

I was now really scared. It wouldn't surprise me if the baby had died. There is so much that needs to go right for a baby to survive, what are the odds that it is all working? How long could it have been dead? What if that last midwife had mistaken my pulse for the baby's heartbeat? What if I were having some kind of early labor — could I still do something to save the baby?

My husband encouraged me to call the nurse line, but I felt like it wasn't okay. There was a small part of me that felt like I was overreacting. Healthy babies are born all the time; it is probably all just fine. There was nothing really wrong. I had some small symptoms but nothing big, no bleeding and no cramping. What was I going to say, "My belt fits better today than it did yesterday?" That sounds like a frantic, off-the-wall pregnant woman.

Finally, I broke down and called, and the nurse was great. She told me it was really normal to be feeling these things, especially for a woman who has had a miscarriage or other major complication. She listened to all my concerns and then invited me to come in the next day to hear the heartbeat.

That was all I needed. Just having called and knowing that within 24 hours I would hear the baby's heart, or not, I began feeling much better. My baby would be either dead or alive, but at least I would now know. For some reason this allowed me to let go of my worry until then. As the day passed, between my calling the nurse line and us going to see the midwife, I began feeling stronger and stronger. By the time my husband and I arrived at the clinic, I felt a lot of emotions inside of me: sadness, love, confusion, fear — but I knew whatever happened I would be okay.

Dawn heard the heartbeat at her midwife appointment and ended up having a healthy baby boy twenty-four weeks later. What pregnant woman wouldn't have fears that her baby was okay? Any pregnant woman can tell you that the relief of knowing the baby is alive and fine by an ultrasound or heartbeat check wears off in about twenty-four hours. With each passing day of no data, the trust that the baby is alive and fine begins to diminish. You could probably graph your rise and fall of fears for the baby in perfect correlation with your healthcare visits.

For Dawn, as for many women, keeping that fear and worry for the safety of the baby stuffed inside just allows it to grow, causing all kinds of fear-based stress. So, as ridiculous as the situation may seem, when you have strong fears or worries about your baby, get some help. Call your healthcare provider and tell him what you are afraid of. Let him reassure you. If that is not enough, schedule an appointment just to hear the baby's heartbeat. Schedule an additional ultrasound if that is what you need to feel confident your baby is forming correctly. Pregnancy is not the time to buck up and take it. You are already taking a lot just going through

the pregnancy. So give yourself permission to take the actions you need to set your mind at ease.

BABY NIGHTMARES AND DAYMARES

These fears or worries for yourself and your baby also seem to periodically invade your dreams. Michelle was really struck by the vividness of a fear that crept into her dreams:

I was three days past my due date, and I just had my first really vivid and scary nightmare about the baby. I woke from this dream, still thinking it was real, and it was only until I realized that I still had this bulging belly with a baby inside that my sense of reality shifted from the dream to the early morning hours in my own bed. I had to wake my husband to tell him about it.

I dreamed that we went to deliver the baby and several blobs of tissue came out, but none of them were the baby. I kept looking to see if the baby were somehow hidden in these blobs of tissue, but I couldn't find it anywhere. The medical people just said that we didn't ever really have a baby.

I was shocked and horrified. Neither my husband nor I could believe it. How could we have waited nine months and have no baby. I felt totally defeated. My mouth just kept gaping open in disbelief. We should have insisted on an ultrasound at twenty weeks. How could this happen? What would we do with our lives to move forward? And all of this stress and stretching of my body with no baby to show for it. This was some kind of cruel joke. Relief was all I could feel when I realized this was only a dream and put my arms around the baby still inside me, waiting to be born.

Although you can't control your dreams, you can do something to keep them from taking control of you. If, or maybe we should say when, you have nightmares centered around your pregnancy:

➤ Find someone with whom to discuss the dream. This keeps it from rolling around in your own head all day, allows you to see it from a different perspective, and may even result in some well-needed support.

➤ Write it down. This is another way to keep the dream from swimming around in your own head. At the same time, this action gives you a chance to review the dream and gain a new perspective.

➤ Look to see if you can identify a fear or worry in the dream that rings true for you. You may have a feeling or fear that is lost down inside or needs some added attention.

➤ Remind yourself it is only a dream and has no more or less meaning than what you choose to give it.

Then there are the baby daymares! These are unpleasant mental escapades that can be spawned by any random occurrence. Sheri experienced them often during her pregnancy:

I was reading an article in a parenting magazine, which told stories of leaving your child alone in a car as a form of parental neglect. It sent my mind off on quite a ride. I imagined I brought my new baby to this big choir I have been participating in. People were excited to see it and one woman asked if she could hold my new baby. I said yes. She carried the baby around and then stepped out of the room. I was uncomfortable with this and inclined to follow her but didn't. When she came back in, she didn't have my baby with her any longer. I ran up to her, asking where my baby was. She denied ever having held my baby. I continued insisting she had the baby and she insisted she did not. I ran out into the hall and there was no sign of my baby out there either. I imagined she had passed the baby on to a person in the hall who was going to sell her.

The whole drama was really unsettling. It was uncomfortable that I had even thought up such a scenario, that my worries were coming out through these kinds of thoughts. It left me realizing just how much I want this baby in my life, how protective I am of it and how important it is to follow my instincts even if they feel a little overprotective.

You have slightly more control over your waking imagination, but it is surprising how quickly your racing thoughts can still get away from you. When you catch yourself spinning such an unsettling tale:

➤ Don't let it fool you into thinking that it is a vision carrying some kind of intuitive message. Remember, it is only thought. All you have to do to put an end to its power is stop thinking about it. Then — poof — it is gone.

➤ Remind yourself that this is normal, that ninety-nine percent of pregnant woman do the same thing and most of them have had successful pregnancies with beautiful, healthy, babies.

➤ Take some time to consider if you have a concern you have either not consciously noticed having had or you have tried to push aside as a ridiculous overreaction. If you find something, take some time to address the concern directly.

FOUR STEPS TO BALANCE YOUR FEARS AND WORRIES

Welcome to the pregnancy club. You realize you're not running this show, and your fears and worries are growing as rapidly as bacteria in a well-fed petri dish. Don't panic, you are still a mature, functioning adult, and this is a normal part of what it means to be pregnant. In fact, having all of this fear is probably the most rational reaction you could possibly have to the reality of another human being coming to life inside of you.

When you realize you are getting emotionally hooked by one or more of your fears and worries, begin by:

1. Letting go of any self-criticism or judgment you may have towards yourself for feeling this "irrational" fear and worry. Remind yourself that it is perfectly normal.

2. Taking some time to understand what is motivating your fears and worries. Ask yourself:

➤ What parts of your pregnancy experience cause the most fear and worry?

➤ When do these fears and worries tend to show up? Is it when you are tired, have down time, talk to a particular person or find yourself in a particular situation?

➤ How do you respond to your fears and worries?

➤ In what ways do you see yourself giving your power over to these fears and worries?

➤ What can you do to regain your power? Get some support, face the fear or reconnect with what is most important to you.

3. Looking to see if the fear or worry has anything useful to offer you. These are often things such as:

➤ Reconnecting you to a part of yourself you have ignored.

➤ Reminding you to build or tap into your support system.

➤ Calling you to let go of your iron grip on control.

➤ Opening your heart to what is most important.

4. Reining in your active imagination. Many of us have a tendency to imagine the worst. Stop thinking about how awful it

could be, and remember that the odds of having a healthy you and a healthy baby at the end of all of this are in your favor. Check in with yourself and see if:

> Your fears or worries are messing with your internal knowing or intuition.

> You need to shift some of your expectation of what it means to be in control.

> You need to remind yourself of the places you do have some control.

> You need to make a special request of your partner during a particularly challenging time.

Finally, if you continue to struggle, see what else you can find out there to help you calm your fears, find the answers you need, deepen your understanding or shift your perspective. Look for books, movies, activities or groups that can assist you in this endeavor.

Fears and worries can have a way of taking over and consuming every ounce of brain space in their host body. Allowing them this kind of latitude will only undermine your strength and make you their prisoner. With a little bit of work, fears and worries can be seen in balance with respect to the other data you have on your current situation.

Summary

What to Do When — POP! — Your Bubble of Control Bursts

Remember, You Will Have to Let Go of:
- The pregnancy you created for yourself in your mind, and instead address the realities your actual pregnancy presents.
- Perceiving every feeling you have as solidly rooted in reality. The feeling is valid, it just may not be the last word on truth.
- Trying to control those situations that are uncontrollable.
- Allowing your feelings to overwhelm you and run your life.
- Getting caught up in the drama you can build out of a challenging situation.

Look for the Opportunity to:
- Diminish the relentless nagging of your pregnancy worries.
- Change your outlook just by perceiving a situation differently.
- Take advantage of the personal power that comes when you stop trying to control the uncontrollable.
- Trust you have what it takes to get back your balance when you lose it in a challenging situation.
- Find the choices within your sphere of control no matter what challenge you are facing.
- Live comfortably with unknowns and not put yourself through so much unnecessary mental torture.

Resources

On Living Without Being in Control

The Tao of Motherhood, Vimala McClure. (Navato, CA: New World Library, 1997.)

End the Struggle and Dance with Life, Susan Jeffers, PhD. (New York, NY: St. Martin's Griffin, 1996.)

On Worry and Fear

How Much Joy Can You Stand?, Suzanne Falter-Barns. (New York, NY: Ballantine Wellspring, 2000.)

Feel the Fear ... and Beyond, Susan Jeffers, Ph.D. (New York, NY: Fawcett Columbine, 1998.)

Facing Fear, Finding Courage: Your Path to Peace of Mind, Sarah Quigley and Mariln Shrayer, Ph.D. (Berkeley, CA: Conari Press, 1996.)

Feel the Fear and Do it Anyway, Susan Jeffers, Ph.D. (New York, NY: Fawcett Columbine, 1987.)

On Inner Strength

One Day My Soul Just Opened Up, Iyanla Vanzant. (New York, NY: Fireside, 1998.)

Conversations with God: An Uncommon Dialogue Book I, Neale Donald Walsch. (New York, NY: G. P. Putnam's Sons, 1996.)

Simple Abundance: A Daybook of Comfort and Joy, Sarah Ban Breathnach. (New York, NY: Warner Books, 1995.)

The Pregnant Woman's Comfort Book: A Self-Nurturing Guide to Your Emotional Well-Being During Pregnancy and Early Motherhood, Jennifer Louden. (San Francisco, CA: Harper San Francisco, 1995.)

On Exploring the Meaning of Your Dreams

The Everything Dreams Book, Trish and Rob MacGregor. (Holbrook, MA: Adams Media Corporation, 1998.)

The Little Giant Encyclopedia of Dream Symbols, Klaus Vollmar (New York, NY: Sterling Publishing Co., Inc., 1997.)

STRATEGY SIX
WATCH FOR OPPORTUNITIES TO BALANCE THE UPS AND DOWNS OF FAMILY LIFE

Most pregnant women and their partners find themselves looking with new interest towards children and the entire concept of family. Well, that's obvious, but in addition, there are some less-than-obvious reactions that are often so intense during pregnancy that they can catch you off guard.

It is likely that your interest in family began growing as you made your decision to get pregnant, unless of course your pregnancy took you by surprise, then you may have some catching up to do. Either way, you are now on your way to creating a new family. Strap yourself in for a life-long adventure.

Looking at the idea of beginning a family and seeing it actually take shape as the contents of your belly fills your horizon are two very different vantage points. One is still relatively hypothetical while the other is teetering on the edge of a new reality. While poised on this edge, you can find yourself experiencing three common reactions to family. They are:

➤ Imagining all of the joy of building a new family with your partner.
➤ Mounting fears at the thought of stepping back into full-time family life.
➤ Realizing the magnitude of entering into the social institution of family.

The bulk of this chapter will focus on building your peace of mind around the whole concept of family, ushering you through the good, bad and even any ugly that can accompany your evolving reactions and getting you prepared for the family life that is coming your way.

Use this foray into family to assist you in clarifying what is important to you. What attributes, norms or values do you want to see as a foundational part of this family you are creating with your new baby? What kinds of roles do you want to play? How do you want to link your baby with your larger family of origin? Let this chapter aid you in consciously choosing and shaping the family you create with your new child. Then use this clarity and take action. Do what is required to ensure you follow through on the beautiful vision you have begun weaving for yourself, your baby, your nuclear family and even your larger, extended family.

All Joy and Infatuation with the Details of Hearth and Home

It can be so wonderful. You are on the threshold of a new life and, if this is something you are ready for, it can be wonderful beyond your wildest dreams. At times, it feels like sheer euphoria. The world is your oyster, and you see it all through the most beautifully tinted, rose-colored glasses you can imagine. From this pregnant perspective every part of your future life with your baby can be cause for celebration! Enjoy every minute of it. And as Nancy found, this jubilant phenomenon pervaded even to the less glamorous aspects of family life with a baby.

I am twenty weeks along in my pregnancy, and I have a total and complete passion about diapers. For some strange reason, of which I have no explanation, I was completely entranced by the idea of using cloth diapers on my baby. Maybe it was the hormones or some fundamental parental urge, but for my family, it just felt more fulfilling and in alignment with my values to use cloth diapers. However, I didn't know the first thing about them.

I began my search by jumping on the Internet. What an experience that turned out to be! The first ten sites I visited were focused on diapers as part of exotic sexual escapades! Not exactly what I had in mind.

But I persevered through the adult forays back to diaperhood and found a site called weebes.com. Here was an expert on how to do your own cloth diapers. She had everything you could imagine wanting or needing. She even had page after page of instructions and directions on how to put them on, take care of the baby's diaper needs, easily handle poopy messes and launder the diapers. I placed my order.

A week later, it all arrived. It was better than Christmas! I quickly opened the boxes and began inspecting all of the items, telling my husband about the role of each in our new baby's life. I immediately began setting it all up in the baby's room, arranging the wet- and dirty-diaper pails, finding locations for the diapers, organizing our desk-turned-changing table. My husband and I were creating a little organization called "our family" and we could set it all up just as we wanted it. It was great fun! I could hardly pull myself away to follow through on any of that day's other commitments. I was definitely an excited mom-to-be!

So now all I need is my baby. I can't wait to put diapers on her. By the time she arrives, I know I will have the diapering down, at least on a stuffed bear.

If it is possible to feel this way about diapers, think about how jubilant you can feel about some of the more desirable aspects of the whole experience. What are your joyful daydreams around creating, participating in and caring for your new family? Is the fulfillment of your dreams achieved:

➤ In providing a loving home?

➤ In caring for this miracle, your baby, that has filled your life?

➤ In entering a new and exciting stage of life?

➤ In doing something totally different than you have ever done before?

➤ In re-entering the intimacy of a family unit?

➤ In giving at a level you never before dreamed of?

➤ In sharing a new phase of your life with your partner?

➤ In committing to another human being in a whole new way?

When you are on the threshold of adding a baby to your family, so much seems possible, and fulfillment can be found in all of the diverse experiences that accompany it.

BASK IN YOUR JOY

This hope-filled family joy is some of the best that life has to offer, and you can bask in it throughout your pregnancy. Even when you are faced with a pregnancy-related challenge, the knowledge that it will end and you will have this beautiful baby in your life allows the spark of this joy to linger. After the birth of your baby, the joy of creating a family together is a second wonderful gift pregnancy has to offer you. Make the most of it. Life after the baby is born won't necessarily look as rosy, so take time to allow yourself to experience such a rich sense of exhilarating anticipation as you await the arrival of your baby. Four ways that you can be intentional about this are to:

Intention One: Stop and Take Notice — There is New Family Joy All Around You. In the busyness of life, your joy may be pushed underground. You're so busy going from one thing to the next that you may not even notice the joy of building a new family swelling

up inside of you. Joy can also be lost in the overwhelming experience of pregnancy. There is so much that is happening to you in such a short time, you just don't notice that, in addition to everything else, there is joy.

With both being busy and overwhelmed, your actual experience of joy may be only the tip of the iceberg. All of the pleasure you could experience may be silently floating under the surface of your awareness. It is just waiting there for you to stop and realize, "Hey, I am creating a new family, and I am the happiest person on the planet!" You may feel many things throughout your pregnancy, but every woman should get to feel top-of-the-world joy many times.

Use the questionnaire below to reveal if you are missing out on some of the joy of this experience. Respond to the twelve statements by marking each as either true or false.

Your Family Joy-o-Meter True or False (T/F)

1. I spend most of my free time thinking about what I have to do next.
2. I feel guilty if I let myself stop "working" and do something I'd call fun or joyful.
3. I have spent most of my pregnancy experience worrying

about myself and the baby.

4. I can't remember the last time I felt joyful.
5. When I do feel joyful, it only lasts for a couple of minutes.
6. I feel joy, but I don't really do anything about it, and then it just passes.
7. I have trouble knowing how to express the joy I feel.
8. When my partner is acting all jubilant, I get uncomfortable and want to bring him back to reality.
9. I often forget that I have a lot to be joyful about.
10. I am too scared to feel joy.
11. I never thought beginning a new family was a joyful event in my life.
12. I feel a degree of joy around the pregnancy, but I know that there is more to be joyful about than I realize.

How may of these statement are true for you? Tally up all of your true responses. Take that number and see where you fall.

0 – 2 Trues. You are likely doing a good job of balancing the challenges of pregnancy with the joys that building a new family has to offer you. Keep it up!

3 – 9 Trues. Turn up your joy-o-meter. You are finding some of the joy that comes with a pregnancy, but there is more of which you can take advantage. Use the information in this chapter to aid you in accessing all of the joy that can be yours during this time.

10 – 12 Trues. Act Fast! There is much family joy you are missing out on. Commit some time today to sit back and notice what makes you happy or joyful about this pregnancy. Do something joyful, even if you don't feel the joy inside. Then look for what has gotten in the way of your ability to experience joy.

Look over each of the statements you marked as true again and see where you find the biggest roadblocks. Keep these blocked areas in mind as you continue reading this chapter.

Intention Two: Indulge with Your Partner. You have picked this wonderful person to spend your life with, and now you are having a baby together. Sure, there may be some day-to-day challenges, but in the big scheme of things, what's not to be joyful about? Help each other remember this. Make sharing joy in your family a part of your pregnancy experience together. Below are some ways you can assist one another in finding and indulging in joy.

➢ Spend some time each day talking about the positive things that happened.

➢ Allow your partner to feel really jubilant, even if you do not.

➢ Make sure you laugh together at least once a day.

➢ Talk with other couples about the joy they felt during their pregnancy or in the weeks after the baby was born.

➢ Help each other remember that sometimes really big feelings of joy about family are expressed in unexpected ways, such as through tears, due to the magnitude; silence, due to the awe; or fear, due to the excitement.

These actions, and others like them, will enable you to connect with one another and your new baby through joy rather than just through the more challenging emotions of pain, struggle, fear or feeling overwhelmed.

Intention Three: Share It with the World Around You. So you feel all this warm glowing joy of building a family bubbling inside of you. Great — now take the lid off and let it fill all of you and spill over onto everyone you meet. Our world can use all of the joy it can get. Think of the spreading of your joy as one of the first positive contributions your baby is making to the planet. Some ways to do this are to:

➢ Smile at people when you make eye contact with them instead of looking away.

➢ Take a couple of moments each day to focus on your joy, let it come to the surface of your awareness and then act on the next opportunity you come across to spread joy.

➢ Check to see that what you are feeling and the face you are projecting out to the world are in alignment. Actually look at yourself in the mirror. Your body language could be expressing complacency, annoyance or boredom. How would it look different if you were to let your body language express the joy that is inside? What impact would that have on everyone with whom you come into contact?

➢ Find room in your life to do something small but memorable for another. Offer a bus-riding colleague a lift on an inclement night or help a harried mother pack her groceries.

➤ Surprise a person you care about by sending an anonymous gift with a thoughtful message.

Think about the impact you have on others as well as your own peace of mind when you let your family joy shine out as far as you can.

Intention Four: Fan the Glow of this Initial Spark. See the joy of pregnancy as kindling for the long-burning flames of joy you build with your family. Right now, this very moment, you, your body and the unknown mystery of life are creating your baby. What a thing to be joyful about. And it is just the beginning. What will it feel like when this little person takes his or her first steps, speaks a first word or sings a first song? What amazing events to witness and with every one the joy you feel is strengthened. Your ability to experience joy now in your pregnancy will lead to the joy you find in life with your new family.

This is not to say that being a part of a family with a baby is a cakewalk. In fact, it is probably one of the hardest things you will ever do. It is tiring beyond compare, but at the same time it is so purposeful and fulfilling. In every way imaginable, creating and then caring for a baby is about living life on all cylinders. It has moments where the rush surpasses even the most extreme of sports. At times, it can be grueling and crushing, and at other times it can be the closest thing to paradise here on earth.

When the World Turns and Your Family Joy is Lost on the Bottom of the Heap

Don't be surprised when you bump into some of the potential realities that can come with living a life full of so much joy. With most ups in life there are downs. Unfortunately, this truth also applies to pregnancy. Some of the potential downs you may find are:

Family Joy Dampened by Having to Wait. Joy and anticipation go hand in hand throughout a pregnancy, and a life filled with these two emotions can be followed by a painful sense of waiting. The same can be said about parts of family life. Elise was excited for the birth of her first child and, with this excitement, she was also very aware of how much waiting she was doing.

I am waiting. It seems like this is the theme of childbearing.

You wait to get pregnant. Then you wait for nine months for it to grow. Then you wait through labor to dilate, and then finally after all that waiting, you get to meet this new person. Nine months is actually quite fast when you consider you are making a person, but I am so ready to meet him or her that it seems as if it is an unbearable eternity.

Yesterday, I woke up feeling lost and depressed. I felt like my life before the baby was winding down and my life with the baby still seemed so far away. I'm almost at thirty-eight weeks, so that means it could still be four weeks before this little person arrives. You say, as my rational self says, four weeks is no big deal, that the baby will be here before you know it. Enjoy these last few weeks without a child. Once this baby comes, your life will never be the same. But my emotional self says, "I feel lost and empty." I have been waiting for this child, and I am ready for it to come now. The possibility of spending another four weeks without it feels so sad. I really want to begin being part of a family. I wish my baby were here now.

I spent a large portion of yesterday crying and feeling empty. I wished I could sit in the rocking chair and just hold our baby. I wished I could feed it, dress it or change its diapers. I am ready for my life with this baby to begin. But I don't get to do anything to make it start. I have to continue waiting.

I have realized one thing that made it hard: I didn't have anything baby-related I could do. It seems to be easier to wait if I can do something to prepare my family for the baby's arrival or buy something we need for the baby. If I cannot have the baby, at least I can feel close by doing something related to the baby. But with nothing baby-related to do, the waiting is harder. I have considered knitting a sweater for this baby, just so I had a way to feel close to it when I had no other baby-related activities.

If you are very aware of waiting for your baby to join your family and see this dampening your joy, some things you can do are:

➤ Get caught up on those "someday" projects that will ultimately benefit your family such as putting pictures in albums, cleaning out old files and sorting out drawers or closets.

> Plan an Overdue Party. Make it a big shindig, it will likely be your last for a while. Have some fun with the fact that maybe there will be a party or maybe there won't, depending on when the baby comes.

> Rent or go see a lot of movies.

> Enlist some friends to take you on an adventure for a day.

If all else fails, resort to the age-old strategy of keeping yourself busy and fill your calendar with activities.

Family Joy Dispersing as Dreams Collide with Reality. During the early stages of pregnancy, budding parents are often enjoying the dreams of family. "We're going to take care of a baby, and it will be so sweet and cuddly and wonderful." This is all true and wonderful to fantasize about. In addition, there is the reality of raising a family, which is often more gooey, sticky and noisy. Sarah has a great story that highlights the collision of her family dream with the potential reality.

My husband and I have gotten into the habit of stopping by the baby's room on our way to bed and tucking in a stuffed moose we bought for our unborn baby. We pat its stomach or poke its big nose and wish it a good night's rest. Then, we usually begin talking directly to our baby, telling it how much we are looking forward to it coming into our lives.

Last night, like many others, we stopped to tuck the moose into bed. As we walked out of the room, my husband began to wail. Waah, he wailed. At first I thought, what in the world is he doing? As he continued, I thought, what a terrible sound, and then I realized this baby is going to cry and it will sound much like this if not worse.

In my dream of building a beautiful family with our baby, I had totally forgotten the reality of babies crying, loudly, often and long. He continued to cry and I noticed how this noise really changed our home, instantly. It filled the space much more than the sweet, little baby room with the colorful paint and the new lamp. Waah, Waaaah. This sound rang through the whole house and there was no escaping the edge it added to the space.

Waaaaaaah, Waaaaaaah, he continued. And I realized I have been living in a dreamland. As if it will be fun to clean poopy diapers, something I will feel good about, similar to eating an apple instead of ice cream. And sure the baby will cry, but in my daydreams, I quickly and calmly sooth the child. But I know this is not reality. This baby will barf all over the bed, poop up more diapers and clothing than I can ever even imagine cleaning, and cry with all the fury it can muster for hours at a time, sending my husband and me to the brink of insanity and back!

How can I face these messy hurdles? I am still trying to figure out how I'm going to make it through labor. When I am pushing this new being out of me and contorting my body in ways I cannot even imagine, I do not want to think about spit up, poop and crying. What kind of motivation would that be? I want to think about wonderful moments together, small little hands and peaceful slumber in my arms. I think I'll just hang on to my fantasy a little longer.

It seems that Sarah has nailed it. Enjoy all of the dreams and fantasies you have about what it will be like to add this new member to your family, and let any reality that is different find you when it needs to. And when it does, remember that reality has a few more ups and downs than the dream of family, but ultimately this real life with your baby will probably exceed any dream you can create. Ask any parent. Most will tell you that the part they play in their family is one of the most fulfilling roles they have ever been granted. Then they will reach for a burp cloth to wipe a freshly deposited blob of spit-up off of the front of their shirt.

The reality is that this family you are creating is monumental. It will forever alter the course of your life, as well as the life of your children and your children's children. Begin to appreciate its impact.

Family Joy Constricted Due to Others' Reactions. For some strange reason, some people in our world are uncomfortable being around a big dose of joy, and they have to try to minimize it or get it into "proper perspective." Such a response may reflect back how little they feel their own joy, they may worry that too much joy can be out of control or they may want to keep everyone prepared for the worst. Whatever motivates this response to joy, it can leave you feeling enveloped within the fog of a gray day. You will know you are dealing with a walking joy-eating black hole when you:

➤ Feel judged by another for expressing your joy. (Such a

judgement is about the judger not you, the judgee!)
➤ Find your own joy causing another to feel worse about herself. You may pick this up nonverbally by the look on her face, an uncomfortable silence or a physical pulling away.
➤ Notice another questioning the "legitimacy" of your joy.

When you experience any of these, remember that suppressing your joy is someone else's script. Throw it away and follow the script that allows you and your family to enjoy all the best that life has to offer. Tanya was shocked when she experienced this negativity from some of the visitors who came to see her at the hospital after her baby was born.

Our baby was just a day old. My husband and I could not believe how beautiful she was. All we wanted to do was sit together, holding our baby girl and take in her miraculousness. It was the most powerful sense of joy I have ever felt, and it blanketed everything else that was going on in the whole world. For us, with this wonderful new baby, life was as perfect as it could be.

We were shocked when a couple of our visitors went on and on about how we should expect her to "give us hell" when we got home. These people had children of their own that they loved very much, but they could not stop telling us how grueling the next couple of weeks were going to be. Finally, I'd had enough. I said firmly that may be, but I don't want to hear about that right now. I just want to enjoy these moments with my baby.

When others are having odd or challenging reactions to your personal joy, choose one of the following actions to keep them from raining on your parade:
➤ Keep smiling!
➤ Choose Tanya's track and politely ask them to put a sock in it.
➤ Use a polite diversion to avoid their negativity like needing to get something to eat, take a nap or run an errand so you stop your interaction with them.
➤ Ask your partner or another close relative to run interference for you.
➤ Change the subject.
➤ Use a doctor's-orders excuse to get yourself (or them) out of the room.

Your joy has the ability to be contagious to all who see it. Don't let another's sour reaction keep you from feeling that joy and sharing it with the world around you.

Mounting Fears at the Thought of Stepping Back into Full-Time Family Life

A second normal reaction to the reality of beginning a family is to see the looming shadow of your family of origin standing between you and all you want to create. This reaction can be particularly strong for expectant parents who did not have positive family experience when they were growing up. It is common to have concerns of repeating old, unwanted patterns from your family of origin. For the moment, stop running from all that might be, and turn to face these fears of original family. From here on out, apply your family energy to something you can run towards rather than away from.

DEFLATING THOSE MOUNTING FAMILY-OF-ORIGIN FEARS

There is not a person alive who does not think about their family of origin as they prepare to care for their new baby and family member. For some, these thoughts turn towards a challenging childhood and the unwanted patterns that went along with it. For others, the focus is on reproducing a perfectly wonderful childhood with a few minor tweaks. Either reaction is completely within normal bounds. This is a natural time for reflection and pursuing a desire to improve upon the childhood you experienced.

More than any other place, unwanted habits or patterns tend to come out most at home. The home is a very private place. Most people can put on a good face for the public. But in the home, where a family spends most of its time together, people's best and, unfortunately, worst can be seen. You didn't have a lot of control over this when you were the child. But now you are the parent, and the norms of this family will be largely set by you. Today, you have a lot of say about the patterns that are created in your new family with your baby. This family can fit all of your own values. It can be a place of your own creation, truly designed just as you and your partner most desire it.

So, how do you get beyond the family bogeyman and to the

hearth of those wonderful homefires of family love? The only way you can have this in a family is by making it a priority, raising your awareness around it and taking the action necessary to establish it as the norm for your family. Decide you want a loving and supportive family and then commit to do what it takes to make it a reality. This is a lifelong project of being aware, noticing and addressing the rough spots. Use the structure below to start gaining some clarity about the family fears that can keep you playing blind man's bluff, eluding what you most desire.

First, address the showstoppers. These are the biggies that families can, unfortunately, find themselves repeating generation after generation. These family-of-origin concerns will need to be dealt with before the next less dramatic layer of building family norms can be addressed. These are the areas where it is key that you spend some time working with a trained counselor or therapist. These issues are too deep to be addressed by simply reading a book or completing something like this process. They are things such as:

➤ Alcoholism
➤ Physical or sexual abuse
➤ Drug addiction
➤ Lingering feelings around a parental separation or divorce
➤ Depression or other mental illness
➤ Parental abandonment

If you have not already addressed your own issues or your leftover family-of-origin concerns in these areas, give yourself, your baby and your whole family a priceless gift and address them now! Your baby's life will be forever better because of it. Turn to the resource section in this chapter to begin your process of locating assistance, or call your healthcare provider for a referral.

Second, create a new definition of normal. You can do this by looking at the norms you create. These are habits or ways family members interact with one another. Just as games have rules of play and countries have customs, families have norms. It is likely that your family of origin had at least some normal ways of behaving that, for whatever reason, you want to do differently with your own family. This may not be because your parents did a bad job. It could be because you are a different person, have some different values or because the times have changed.

Some of the norms you can make a conscious decision about are listed below. Each norm is presented as its challenge or limitation to your family vs. its benefits to your family. This allows you to identify what you do not want to recreate and then provides a positive alternative for which you can strive. Look through the list and identify the one or two norms of which you want to be particularly conscious as you build your family. Then, carefully consider the questions underneath to gain insight into your personal truths or challenges accompanying this norm. When answering these questions, base your responses on your interactions with members of your current family, as well as your family of origin. Be honest with yourself. Consider talking through these questions with your partner.

Not listening vs. taking the time to hear and be heard
1. What gets in your way of really listening to the people you care about?
2. What negative messages do you have about listening?
3. What are you giving to your family when you stop and listen on all levels: the words, the body language and what is implied behind both?

Working all the time vs. taking time out to play as a family
1. What do you gain by working (either around the house or at your job) all of the time?
2. When do you give yourself permission to play?
3. What kind of playing will you want to do with your new family?

Being exclusive or judgmental vs. being inclusive and accepting individual differences
1. How do you benefit from your judgements?
2. How are you limited by your judgements?

3. What do your judgements of family members say about you?

4. What impact will your judgements have on your baby as she grows up?

5. In what ways are these judgements restricting your family?

6. What will allow you to set down these judgements ?

Blaming one another vs. taking responsibility and requesting others do the same

1. What impact does blame have on you?

2. What do you do to contribute to blame?

3. What does it look like when the members of a family take responsibility?

4. Where does your baby need you to take responsibility?

Each person for himself or herself vs. looking out for one another and ensuring everybody's needs will be met.

1. What drives you to buy into either of these paradigms?

2. Where is the challenge for you in believing everyone's needs will be met?

3. Describe how it would look if you came home with your baby and every family member's needs were met.

Disrespectful fighting vs. complete avoidance of fighting vs. respectful fighting

1. What does respectful fighting mean to you?

2. How would your baby benefit from growing up in a family that practiced respectful fighting?

3. What one thing would you need to change in how you currently fight with your partner to allow for respectful fighting?

4. How will you make that change?

If you are truly committed to putting those norms you selected in place with your new family, it is important you begin thinking about them now. These norms are not habits you can change in a week or a month. They take time, focus and self-discipline, so begin strengthening these muscles now, while you are still pregnant or still caring for a newborn baby. Then you will be on track by the time your child is old enough to really notice what you are doing, which, by the way, happens much sooner than you'd think.

Third, to reduce your family of origin fears, commit to make it different! This commitment will affect your whole life, as well as that of your children, so make it one you stick to. You have uncovered what is important, and you have told yourself you will do it differently. Then real life enters. The baby cries, you have an argument with your partner, your job gets really stressful and all of a sudden you see yourself falling into all you didn't want to be doing. What can you do when you catch yourself falling short of your commitment?

> ➤ Recommit to yourself, as well as to others, through your actions.
> ➤ Tell someone close to you about the struggles you are having.
> ➤ Stop blaming the job, the disposition of the baby or your partner. Take responsibility for your own unwanted actions.
> ➤ Apologize.
> ➤ Find and take advantage of a resource such as a book, TV show, training seminar, counselor or coach that addresses the topic in some way.
> ➤ Identify and do one thing that is in alignment with the habit you want to build.
> ➤ Identify a reminder or emotional reset that you can use to keep yourself on track. This could be putting a Band-Aid on your finger, identifying a common action, such as blowing your nose, that you can use to remind yourself of your commitment or identifying a place on your body, like your heart, that you can touch when you need to reaffirm your efforts.

It would be so much easier if all you had to do was commit once and know it was done. But, unfortunately, for most people, that is just not how it is. You have to commit, catch yourself going the wrong way and recommit. Do this cycle again and then once more before it starts to become a normal part of your daily life. Don't let this natural process of changing a habit discourage you. Instead, use it as an opportunity to see the importance, reconfirm your desire and go at it again.

Stepping into the Institution of Family

Good, bad or ugly, it is still family — the institution has its pluses and minuses, but overall it is a basic human response to want to live at some level within the context of family. Whether we can see it for ourselves or not, belonging to some form of a family is one of our more intense longings. Family is a powerful force for individuals, a building block for communities and a sustaining link for our nation. It has the potential to be a place where we can experience the most intimate bonding and the warmest sense of acceptance. It is families to which the majority of businesses market, whom politicians target and nonprofit organizations serve. Whatever our opinions of all of this, we are surrounded by it every day. So, in addition to joy and fear, a third very normal reaction to family may be an awakening to the fact that you are becoming an active part of this front-and-center institution. You are stepping into a new role in our society and your awareness of this is a true rite of passage. Welcome! You are in great company.

Family is an institution that tends to remain stable over time; however, the attitudes and ideas people have about it seem to change within the span of a generation. Currently, we are in a time wherein family is gaining importance. The pendulum is shifting from a minority of people placing family first to a time of family renewal. More and more people are again attending to the value of family

and the benefits it provides to all its members and society at large. It is now quite common for parents to put family concerns above career on the priority list. More moms (or dads) are staying home to raise the children, people are passing on big promotions that would get in the way of family time and more people are looking for ways to work from home. All of this puts family first.

What are your current attitudes about family? What do you notice as you take your first few steps into the institution of family? How do you see yourself blending or conflicting with this institution?

There are some common new awarenesses people begin to notice when looking at the world from within the embrace of family. They are:

A New Attitude. The first is that you begin to see a shift in your opinions and attitudes around things relating to family. For example, you may now have a greater interest in schools and paying the taxes necessary to keep them strong. You see the need to provide toys that are fun as well as developmentally appropriate, or issues about child safety may become paramount. Suddenly, you realize the grueling job of raising children as a single parent, you know firsthand how important emergency shelters are, and you want to make it a federal law that all babysitters attend first aid training. You have become one of the many watchdogs driven to protect our next generation. To what new causes have you turned your attention now that you're in the family way?

Falling in Step with Father Knows Best. The second unavoidable awareness is that you now find the media bombards you with role models for behaving as the loving mother, supportive father or perfect family. Before you were part of a family it was all about being free, doing it your own way and blazing your own trail. Now the social message turns 180 degrees.

Be the good, loving mom, keep the house neat and clean, smile at and cuddle your children all of the time, be available to your kids, look great with your two-week-old infant and do it all with no internal strife. Be the fun and reliable dad, do silly things — it's okay if you're absent-minded — and bring home treats. Be the happy family, spend your free time together, happily do household projects together, share fulfilling dinners as a family at the end of a long day, and enjoy each other all living together in peace and harmony. If only it were all truly so beautiful.

There is nothing fundamentally wrong with any of these portraits, other than the fact that they are very one-dimensional and virtually impossible to maintain for more than twenty minutes within the context of any real family. Life just isn't packaged this way.

If you get caught thinking this is what family life should be all, or at least most, of the time, you can find yourself disappointed. The above can all be true some of the time, but so can:

> Crabby babies who cry most of the night.
> Dinners that are far from relaxing and lead you to question the evening meal as a mainstay of family life.
> Parents who are in a conflict.
> Homes that are so messy they could be quarantined.
> Moms who, after three days, still don't have time for a shower.
> Dads who feel burdened by work that never ends.

Just notice that what our culture feeds us about family can be a setup, and see it as just one sliver of the whole truth behind a very powerful and diverse experience.

Passing Along the Cash. A third interesting awareness, as you spend time within the boundaries of this institution, is that you begin to gain, attain and earn money not as much for yourself but for your family. Suddenly, it is all about something larger than yourself. This family has become your cause. Some common examples of this are:

> Watching your personal expenditures fall to the bottom of the wish list after things for the baby or the family as a whole.
> Getting more excited about buying new outfits for the baby than for yourself.
> Beginning to save more a month than you ever did before, all in your child's college fund, of course.
> Asking new questions before deciding to make a big purchase, such as, is it good for the family?

It is likely that in your pregnant state this has already begun occurring.

Where Is the I in Family? This springboards us to a fourth awareness. With all this family, your own individual identity begins to be blurred. When people ask how you are, you tell them about the latest development in your pregnancy or new thing your baby did. You are no longer a single entity, you are a representative from this group called "your family." This can be kind of cool and kind of uncomfortable all at once. The coolness comes from belonging to a group of people in a way that you never have before. You chose these people, and now you are linked together in a powerful way. You are all building a life together. It is a very fulfilling sense of belonging.

As you move from pregnancy into full-time parenthood, this belonging can also get uncomfortable. There will likely be a moment when you lift your head up and realize that in your enthusiasm for belonging to and building your new family, you have forgotten some of what it means to just be you. Some things you can do to keep ahold of your you-ness in all of this family love is to:

> ➤ Find something that is yours, some reason to leave the family unit and attend to a commitment that has nothing to do with the family.
> ➤ Take a weekend away from home without any other family members.
> ➤ Plan a day at home all alone.
> ➤ Look back in your journal and read from a time in your life before you were a member of this family.

Every time you notice you have lost sight of your sense of you-ness, even if it is in a small way, take some action to reacquaint yourself with you again. Your baby will grow up and then it will be just you and your partner. In this skinned-down family unit, you will have a lot more time with yourself again. Over the coming years, don't let your relationship with yourself go so far away that it is terribly hard to find later in life.

The Passing of the Family Baton. A final common awareness is that this institution, which seemed like something built for your parents, is becoming yours. You are now one of the many keepers designing what it means to be a family today in our society. The decisions you make about how to raise your family will have all kinds of implications upon how our culture views family and on the state of the institution when your children take it over. How does it feel to take some ownership of shaping this cultural icon?

Use this awareness to motivate you and your partner to be conscious about what you are creating. Here are some questions to help you raise your consciousness as you begin your family.

> ➤ In your mind, what is the best your family can offer to all of its members?
> ➤ What challenges do you and your partner face in building your new family together?
> ➤ What do you want to get from this family?
> ➤ What do you want to give to it?

➤ What will this family require from you?

Think about taking the institution of family further during your stay within its ever-changing boundaries. What could you bring to the act of living within a family that will enrich the experience for those to come? Some things to consider are:

➤ Creating time to just be together. Stop rushing from activity to activity and just be in one place all together on a regular basis.

➤ Having fun together and laughing as much as you can.

➤ Enjoying the influence you have within this family and really stepping into that with passion and gusto.

➤ Looking to those special aunts, uncles or grandparents that can enrich your family with meaningful traditions from the past.

➤ Taking advantage of the mundane daily acts to create a beautiful sense of intimacy and acceptance for all family members.

➤ Redefining the definition of who makes up a family.

➤ Sharing friends together by including your friends in family activities or making friends with another family whom you all enjoy.

As you enter this institution, stop often and notice what meaning it offers to its residents. Commit yourself to build a beautiful place from which to honor all that was in your family of origin and all that can be in this new family you are creating. Help your family to change and grow, as its members require.

However you decide to walk within this framework of family, do it in a way that leaves the institution stronger and more healthy for the next generation. And, most of all, be in the moment with your family and enjoy each stage as it comes. You and your babies will be the better for it.

Summary

Wrestling with Your Own Reactions to Family

Family Can Have You Pinned to the Mat When You Are:
➤ Tapping into your family-related fears or stresses.
➤ Feeling tentative about what it means to be entering the institution of family.
➤ Nervous about how you will break some negative norms from your family of origin.
➤ Limiting the joy of family that could be filling your life.
➤ Realizing that for the sake of you and your unborn baby you need to deal with any addiction, abuse, depression or divorce issues that could limit the health and loving development of your new family.

You and Your Family Can Enjoy a True Sense of Victory When You Are:
➤ Reconnecting around new common interests with extended family members.
➤ Imagining all the joys of life with your new family.
➤ Trusting you have what it takes to build a healthy and secure family life for your new baby.
➤ Finding a new sense of bonding with the current members of your nuclear family.
➤ Consciously choosing all the best from your childhood to recreate within your new family.

Resources

On Family

Family: A Celebration of Humanity, Geoff Blackwell. (Cahners Business Information, Inc., 2001.)

I Only Say This Because I Love You: How the Way We Talk Can Make or Break Family Relationships Throughout Our Lives, Deborah Tannen. (New York, NY: Random House, 2001.)

The Shelter of Each Other: Rebuilding Our Families, Mary Bray Pipher. (Ballantine Books, 1997.)

Making Peace with Your Parents: The Key to Enriching Your Life and All Your Relationships, Leonard Felder and Harold H. Bloomfield. (Ballantine Books, 1996.)

"Because I Said So!": 366 Insightful and Thought-Provoking Reflections on Parenting and Family Life, John Rosemond. (Kansas City, MO: Andrews McMeel Publishing, 1996.)

The Family in the Western World from the Black Death to the Industrial Age, Beatrice Gottlieb. (Oxford University Press, 1993.)

On Joy

Mrs. Sharp's Traditions: Perceiving Victorian Family Celebrations of Comfort and Joy, Sarah Ban Breathnach. (New York, NY: Scribner, 2001.)

Eat Mangoes Naked: Finding Pleasure Everywhere and Dancing With the Pits, Sark. (New York, NY: Fireside, 2001.)

How Much Joy Can You Stand?: A Creative Guide to Facing Your Fears and Making Your Dreams Come True, Suzanne Falter-Barns. (New York, NY: The Ballantine Publishing Group, 1999.)

Simple Abundance: A Daybook of Comfort and Joy, Sarah Ban Breathnach. (New York, NY: Warner Books, 1995.)

Celebrating Joy: Catching the Thieves that Steal Your Joy, Luci Swindoll. (Navpress, 1989.)

On Addiction

Sober for Good, Anne M. Fletcher and Frederick B. Glaser. (Boston, MA: Houghton Mifflin Co., 2001.)

The Thinking Person's Guide to Sobriety, Bert Pluymen. (Griffen Trade Paperback, 2000.)

Kill the Craving: How to Control the Impulse to Use Drugs and Alcohol, Joseph Santoro PhD., Alfred Bergman, Robert Deletis and Joe Santoro. (New Harbinger Publications, 2001.)

The Anonymous Press, www.anonpress.org
A group of AA members focused on making the information
of AA available to all who need it. Phone: (800) 800-4398
Address: PO Box 1212, Malo, WA 99150.

On Abuse

*Allies in Healing: When the Person You Love Was Sexually
Abused as Child,* Laura Davis. (New York, NY:
HarperPerennial, 1991.)

*The Right to Innocence: Healing the Trauma of Childhood
Sexual Abuse,* Beverly Engel. (Ivy Books, 1991.)

Voices, www.voices-action.org
An international organization providing assistance to victims
of incest and child sexual abuse. Phone: (847) 753-9273.

On Depression

The Noonday Demon: An Atlas of Depression, Andrew
Solomon. (New York, NY: Scribner, 2001.)

The Beast: A Journey Through Depression, Tracy Thompson.
(Plume, 1996.)

*How You Can Survive When They're Depressed: Living and
Coping with Depression Fallout,* Anne Sheffield. (New York,
NY: Crown Publishers, 1999.)

Depression Fallout, www.depressionfallout.com
Information for people living with and loving those struggling
with depression.

Postpartum Support International, www.postpartum.net
A social support network, information center and research
guide concerning postpartum mood disorders and depression.

On Divorce

The Unexpected Legacy of Divorce: A 25-Year Landmark Study,
Judith S. Wallerstein, Sandra Blakeslee and Julia M. Lewis. (New
York, NY: Hyperion, 2001.)

The Love They Lost: Living With the Legacy of Our Parent's Divorce,
Stephanie Staal. (New York, NY: Dell Publishing, 2000.)

Strategy Seven

Make New Friends and Consciously Choose What You Want to Do with the Old

You will likely find that some of your friendships will be different after the birth of your baby. It isn't wrong or bad that your friendships rebalance and evolve. It's just that it can be uncomfortable, frustrating, complicated, sometimes exciting and often disorienting. As you already know too well, pregnancy is a time where a lot is coming and going in your life. All of this personal movement will definitely carry over in some way to the friendships you have. When friends are also family members or are going through their own significant life changes, this time of shuffling friends can be even more interesting.

Whether you're pregnant or not, the quality of your friendships directly affects the quality of your life. A life without good friends is less than complete. It is missing a fulfilling component. Contentment is often found in the company of good friends, and the afterglow of those times together can warm your heart and fill you will the richness of connection for days to come. During pregnancy, the value of good friends can be even more magnified.

Building these good friendships may require the investment of attention, the courage to let go or the willingness to put forth new effort. But every investment you make will give back that much more support for you and your unborn child. At this point in your life, you have the opportunity to build a foundation of friendships that will add to your peace of mind and support you through your pregnancy and beyond.

There are many reasons that pregnancy is a natural time for a rebalancing of your friendships. Some common examples are:

➤ You want friends with whom you can talk about the pregnancy and your new life as a parent. Not all friends are interested in lingering over the gory details.

➤ You are interested in new issues, and your past friends just don't get it.

➤ Your physical and mental availability is different than it was before you were pregnant. You are more tired or you are not as available as you once were.

➤ You may bore your old friends with the topic that is consuming your every waking moment. Your friend may just not be able to relate to the whole experience you are having, and your infatuation with it may not be of any interest to him or her.

➤ You may find your friendship was built upon doing things you can no longer do. Such things may be highly aggressive physical activities, extreme sports, drinking alcohol or smoking.

Things are going to have to change to make room for your baby in your life. This includes friends. Here is your chance to be intentional about what you are doing. Where are you headed and what is your future with your friends?

Some Friends Stay the Same

Some friendships will weather this time well with little change. This steadfastness may be a random fluke, your lives may be making similar changes at the same time or it may be a person with whom you have a very close connection. Some actions you can take to maintain consistency with these friends are to:

➤ Be honest and open about any changes taking place between you.

➤ Set up a regular time to talk either over the phone or in person.

➤ Be open to find new activities you can do together that fit your new lifestyle.

➤ Ask your important friends what they like the most about the friendship they have with you and let them know what they mean to you.

➤ Set up a special event with each other.

Some Friends Go Away

In all of life there is a natural process of taking in and letting go. Although there are exceptions, for most of us, the taking in is more fun and the letting go is much more uncomfortable.

Big life transitions are often the times when our friendships evolve. Think back to another big change in your life, such as going to college or changing jobs, what impact did those past life changes have on your friendships?

So how do you know if a particular friendship is shifting and it is time to do some letting go? Here are some flags to help you spot a friendship that may be in transition.

➤ You feel too busy to stay in contact with this person.

➤ This friend has stopped calling or including you in activities.

➤ You consistently leave an interaction with this friend feeling empty or lonely.

➤ You regularly have begun to find yourself feeling bored when you spend time together.

Your answers to these questions give you some insight into which relationship(s) you need to release. It is clearly in front of you now, so take some action. Even if this action is a simple little baby step, it is a beginning.

STEP BY STEP TOWARDS LETTING GO

Sometimes the only letting go you need to do is about a specific part of the friendship. You may keep some parts of your friendship that are still working and let another part go. Or, let go of all that you used to do and begin doing something you never did before that is a better fit for both of you. In doing this, don't compromise too far, you are choosing how you want to keep this person in your life and spend the shrinking time you have available to be with friends. Consider these options in refocusing this friendship.

➤ One-on-one time with each other

➤ Time as couples with your partners

➤ Time in a group

➤ Unscheduled, spontaneous time together

➤ Spending bigger life or family events together

➤ Time on the phone and little or no face-to-face time

➤ Simply exchanging holiday cards

What are you unconsciously doing with your friends just because it is what you've always done? What new forms do your friendships need to take? How would you like to spend your time with each of your friends? Where are you kidding yourself and you really need to set this person free?

It can be hard to manage a long-term friendship that is now distancing. People can easily feel hurt or judged. But if you can make the situation less personal, you may be able to see it as a natural distancing or rebalancing given the changes in your or your friend's life. Letting go can be hard, but dragging on with something that doesn't work for either of you can ultimately be worse.

BEING EXCLUDED AND EXCLUDING YOURSELF

One of the biggest struggles with undoing friendships is that you or your friend walk away from it feeling left out or excluded. One of the realities of pregnancy that can lead to these feelings of exclusion is when you are in a friendship wherein one party is pregnant and the other party cannot get pregnant. Bobby had no

idea this was the stumbling block in her friendship with Cynthia.

Cynthia and I were both in a group of friends that got together for happy hour. Everyone was really a friend with everyone else, and we all did a lot of socializing outside of our monthly happy hour. I got pregnant after a couple years of this happy hour ritual, and I knew Cynthia and her partner were trying to get pregnant, so I worked really hard to be sensitive to her situation. I didn't really talk much about my pregnancy with her, and I spent a lot of time talking with her about how the infertility process was going. We had talked and talked about getting together for dinner just the two of us, and I kept trying to schedule it but it just never quite fit, or, if we did get a time, she would call up and cancel. She was doing all kinds of things with the other women from the happy hour, and I began to feel really bad. I figured she just didn't like me. Finally,

I told her I felt like we didn't have the friendship I wanted and didn't know what to do about it, and she told me that it was hard for her to spend time with me because I was pregnant. I wish she would have just said that earlier rather than putting me off.

No matter how sensitive you both are, when you are pregnant and a friend painfully wants to be pregnant, too, it can quickly lead to hard feelings on both sides.

If you can talk about these differences with each other, you can lessen the feelings of exclusion on all sides. Now, the shifts in your friendships are about the changes taking place in your lives and not about either of you personally.

With some friends, this will not be a conversation you can have, the relationship is just not that close. When that is the case, you will have to do your best to help your friend understand the changing demands on you. And, in turn, you will have to trust and believe any exclusion you feel from him or her is not about you doing it wrong, being a bad friend, becoming a boring person or being unlovable. Instead, chalk it up to the situation.

Throughout all of this, watch for the temptation to slip into a poor-me attitude. Try not to see yourself as somehow victimized by this friendship, personally hurt or stepped upon. Any of these perspectives on a changing friendship serves no one. Some signs that you may be heading towards a poor-me moment are:

➤ Noticing yourself wanting to blame others for what is happening to the friendship, as if it were their fault.

➤ Looking for hurtful motivations on the part of your friend.

➤ Expecting your friend to take care of you and meet all of your expectations.

No matter what the circumstances of this friendship, you never have to be a victim to it. Shake the poor-me's off by talking it through with another person close to you, examining how you have set yourself up to blame your friend or shame yourself and, finally, engaging in some activity that gets you back into your own place of personal power, such as physical exercise, writing in a journal, doing something kind for someone else, signing up for a new adventure or rereading a writing that has personal meaning for you.

A FRIENDSHIP-ENDING GUIDE

When you find yourself becoming clear that it is time to move away from a friendship, use the guide below to assist you in ensuring you do it in the best way possible for the sake of your friend and yourself.

First, depersonalize it. Remind yourself that there is a good chance this is not about you and whether or not you are a good friend. In fact, it probably has nothing to do with who you are and is about the fact that you and/or your friend is changing and want different things. Your lives are beginning to take different paths, and you are both still good people.

Second, take time to mentally decide what you need to do about this friendship. Does your decision make you feel:

➤ Relieved?

➤ Sad?

➤ Depressed?

➤ Confused or wondering why?

What do these feelings mean to you? What do you think this reaction has to tell you? Use your reaction to guide the actions you take. For example, if you feel relieved at the thought of finally being done trying so hard, that is a great sign you are on the right path. However, if the thought of ending the friendship just makes you sadder, then you may need to take a different course of action. Maybe you should have a clear-the-air conversation or just reduce the number of times you see one another.

Third, begin by considering the path of least resistance. You may both be growing away at the same time, and it may be appropriate to do nothing. Just don't call anymore and let the friendship slip off your now-overflowing plate. They don't call, you don't call, and life evolves. You don't need to make a big statement about this transition, unless, of course, you really do feel the need to make a big statement about the friendship.

Fourth, carefully consider the big statement you need to make. What do you really need to do to be able to let go of what was? What do you feel you owe this person given the past you have shared together? What will allow you to walk away from this person feeling unburdened and as if you have a clean slate from which to move forward into your future?

Fifth, remember you have no idea what will happen in the future and that this could be the end of the friendship or just a temporary pause. Donna experienced an old friend coming back into her life when she was pregnant with her second child.

Amie and I had been friends from way back in elementary school. I switched schools at seventh grade and we quickly lost touch. I cannot even really remember how the friendship ended. Over the years, I have often wondered about Amie, what life she was living and where she was. Then one day, totally out of the blue, I received an email from her. She had seen my name and number on a referral list. We quickly exchanged life stories, found out we were in a similar place with children and started getting together with our kids on a regular basis.

The same story could be written about two friends who rediscover each other after the children have grown up. Babies at the same time can bond friendships back together and babies at different times can shake them apart.

No matter how the future actually turns out, take care not to burn a bridge, and reach out again to this person if it makes sense at some point along the way. Throughout it all, remember that both of you are doing the best you know how.

Whatever kind of ending you face with a friend, take some time to be thoughtful about the process you are going through with her. Honor or recognize what this person has brought into your life. What is it she has contributed to you? What impact has she had on you? You can just do this in your own head. Or, if it fits the relationship, give her this acknowledgement directly by sending a heartfelt card or talking over a good meal. Let this friendship end with little or no resentment or leftover baggage for either party. Your attention to this ending process now will allow you to continue on without nagging burdens into the future. Do all you can to keep your relationships simple and clean in this way, and your emotional weight will be a thousand pounds lighter. Pregnant or not, who can't appreciate that?

Some New Friends Show Up

And now, just when you think you have no room for another thing in your life, this wonderful new person, who shares so many of your current interests or experiences, shows up and all of a sudden you are finding space for him or her. Pregnancy is also a time of being drawn to new people and building new relationships, many of which will be there to support you as you adjust to life with your new baby. You may find that you:

> Get really excited to find another pregnant woman or someone with a new baby in your neighborhood.

> Meet another pregnant couple in one of your pregnancy classes with whom you and your partner share interests.

> Meet a really cool pregnant woman in the waiting room at your clinic.

> Connect with a co-worker with whom you have not had much contact in the past.

Take these wonderful new people into your life. They are a great gift, people who have new energy and excitement for you and your pregnancy. The age-old saying is really correct. Make new friends but keep the old, one is silver and the other gold. New or old, each has something unique to offer you.

What Do You Want From Friends?

Whether or not you feel the need to makes some changes in whom you spend your time with, pregnancy is a good time to pause for a moment and consider what you want from your friends. It is likely that what you wanted from your friendships before you were pregnant and what you want now looks a bit different. Step back and consider what those differences are. Then take the necessary actions so you get what you want from your friends, and help these people be the best possible friends they can during this enormously important time in your life. Everyone wants different things from friendships; what do you want?

What Do You Want to Give?

What do you have time and energy to give to your friends? And to whom exactly do you want to be giving it? Most friendships don't just materialize; it takes some attending to from both parties. This

means some effort on your part is required in the form of:
- ➤ Telephone calls.
- ➤ Time together and making room in your busy schedule for one another.
- ➤ Empathy for one another, even if it is not a situation to which you totally relate.
- ➤ Paying attention to those things that are very important to the other person.
- ➤ Allowing yourself to be influenced at some level by this person, appreciating things he or she loves or taking the time to really acknowledge his or her stand on an issue.
- ➤ Openness for differences between you.
- ➤ Honesty about who you are.
- ➤ Flexibility. They may cancel plans at the last minute or be in a bad mood on occasion, and, as a friend, this, on an infrequent basis, is taken in stride.

All of these are ways you can be giving in your friendships. You don't usually have to do a lot. You can forget birthdays, cancel dates and even tell them you are too busy to get together and still be a great friend. It is all about doing it with love and care. So how do you want to be giving as a friend? Where do you see yourself falling short these days? How has your pregnancy impacted who you are as a friend? What could you do right now to let your closest friends know you really care?

What Do You Want to Get?

Friendship is a place for giving as well as receiving. So when you are on the receiving end, what would you like? Some common things pregnant women look for in their friends are:
- ➤ Someone to listen to your thoughts, reflections and concerns.
- ➤ A person with similar philosophies on pregnancy and ideas on parenting and family.
- ➤ A companion who can challenge your self-imposed limitations in a gentle and loving way.
- ➤ Someone fun to hang out with who makes you laugh.
- ➤ One who has been through all of this pregnancy stuff before.
- ➤ A source of emotional support, someone you can call when you are in the height of an emotionally sad, scared or angry place.

➤ Your personal fountain of pregnancy information. However, watch out with this one, sometimes this person can become a source of misinformation. Sally found this out towards the end of her first pregnancy.

Kim, one of my best friends, already has three kids, so it has been great to call her with all of my questions. Usually, she has been right on, but towards the end of my pregnancy, my baby began to move a lot less and she told me that was normal because there is less room in the womb. That sounded plausible, so I didn't worry about it. But when I casually mentioned this to my midwife, a week later, she jumped into action. She quickly checked for a heartbeat, had the baby's movements monitored for an hour, and did an unscheduled ultrasound. Everything was just fine, but this lack of movement in my unborn baby was clearly a big concern.

What else do you want from friends? Think about your current cast of friends; are you getting all that you want from them? Where are the gaps?

If you find you do have a gap, a desire from friends that is not currently met, decide to take some action. Depending upon what gap you are facing, you could:

➤ Make a request of an existing friend.

➤ Look for a new friend by striking up a conversation with that interesting pregnant woman you recently met or signing up for a class that will attract the kind of friend you are seeking.

➤ Look up an old friend with whom you have lost contact.

➤ Ask your other friends if they have a friend who has what you want and set yourself up on a "blind date."

➤ Join an organized group that could fill that gap and also fits with your interests or your future life with your baby.

➤ Consider a family member who may fit the friendship bill.

Commit to take one action to address your friendship gap and get the aspects of friendship that are missing back into your life.

Your friends understand that your life is really full right now. They know that your focus is on preparing for your baby. They can give you a lot of latitude, yet at the same time, they want to know you still care. In addition to having your baby, you still need your friends, so make a commitment to do some things to keep these connections strong.

Summary

***The Ups and Downs of Adding a Pregnancy
to Your Friendships***

The Gold and Silver of Friendships During Pregnancy
- ➤ Your relationship with one or more of your current friends is forever strengthened through your pregnancy.
- ➤ You build a pregnancy supported by a foundation of unconditional friendship.
- ➤ You have a new friend who is as interested in diapers, strollers and bottles as you are.
- ➤ You have made an effort and intentionally chosen to keep these wonderful friends as active participants in your life.
- ➤ You find a deepening or newfound honesty in a current friendship.
- ➤ You risk an open conversation and move a friendship to a new and better place.

The Friendship Challenges You Can Face
- ➤ Your relationship with one or more of your current friends will never again be as close.
- ➤ Your conversations with a friend are not as interesting, fulfilling or fun as they used to be.
- ➤ You leave a friend feeling misunderstood, judged, bored, cut-off or ignored.
- ➤ You just don't have the time or space to stay in touch with a friend in the way you used to.
- ➤ You sense a close friend is distancing himself or herself from you.
- ➤ You wake up to the fact that you have gotten stuck unconsciously doing things with this person because it is what you have always done.

Resources

On Friendship

Connecting: The Enduring Power of Female Friendship, Sandy Sheehy. (New York, NY: William Morrow & Company, 2000.)

Girlfriends, Jayne Wexler and Lauren Cowen. (Philadelphia, PA: Running Press Book Publishers, 1999.)

A Good Friend: Ten Traits for Enduring Ties, Les Parrott. (Ann Arbor, MI: Servant Publications, 1998.)

Friends for the Journey, Madeline L'Engle and Luci Shaw. (Ann Arbor, MI: Servant Publications, 1997.)

Friendshifts: The Power of Friendship and How It Shapes our Lives, Jan Yager Phd. (Stanford, CT: Hannacroix Creek Books, Inc., 1997.)

The Friendship Factor, Alan Loy McGinnis. (Minneapolis, MN: Augsburg Publishing House, 1979.)

52 Ways to Celebrate Friendship, Lynn Gordon. (San Francisco, CA: Chronicle Books, 1999.)

Strategy Eight
Find Your Way to
Gentleness with Your Spouse

By entering into a pregnancy together, you have thrown a very new, consuming obsession right in the middle of your relationship, and it can cause all kinds of stresses for you and your partner, adding marital conflict to the list of things shrinking your peace of mind. With a pregnancy, your relationship is changing in many ways. The two of you may now have:

➤ An increase in your interdependence with one another.

➤ A different kind of sexual experience with one another.

➤ New types of conversations.

➤ A new set of activities in your life together.

➤ New fears about each other, the relationship and life with your new baby.

➤ Bigger demands pushing your ability to communicate with one another to the limits.

➤ A new mix of household responsibilities.

➤ New levels of commitment to one another.

See these changes for what they are, a necessary and natural part of the pregnancy process, and you can keep from falling into the trap of fighting about why life is not like it used to be.

Your relationship has a lot on its plate right now. You can help it along by watching out for those relationship toxins — your own unconscious assumed expectations. Pregnancy is a prime environment for these unwanted, insidious expectations to take hold in the minds of either partner and wind their way into the core of your relationship. Some of the common expectations that can really tangle you up are:

➤ Assuming that just because your life together has always

been a certain way that it will continue to be so through the pregnancy and on into parenthood.

➤ Believing that because you are having a baby together, everything has changed and you should no longer fight or disagree with one another. As if this could ever be true, but now with the addition of the baby, it is such an important time, it should be different, right? Wrong!

➤ Thinking that now your partner should be there for you one hundred percent of the time.

➤ Believing that now that you are building a family together, your partner should be able to meet all of your new needs and wants.

➤ Feeling entitled to something and not openly asking for it.

Expecting any of this during your pregnancy is a setup for disappointment.

It can be a challenge to acknowledge that you're maintaining one or more of these expectations, let alone convincing yourself to let go of them. But by tuning into your self-awareness, checking in at a gut level, letting go of those expectations of how it should be, and committing to build a new definition of normal life with your spouse, you will make your entire pregnancy experience much easier on both of you. Shift your focus towards what you both want and follow that up with new routines that allow you to make the best possible choices in each circumstance. Now, you are well on your way to enjoying the peace of mind that comes with a relationship in flux but not in turmoil. With that, here are some tools to help you address these major transitions pregnancy introduces into a relationship and begin to turn assumed expectations into clearly stated wants and choices.

Who Is Supposed to Do the Dishes Around Here?

One thing that can do a lot for keeping peace and serenity within the boundaries of your relationship is reducing any feelings of chaos and clutter, being taken for granted, or frustration and resentment. Believe it or not, many of these deep-seated feelings can be resolved by the simple act of deciding together who is responsible for specific domestic tasks and when they are to be completed.

Many couples live prepregnant life by assuming household tasks will just happily get done as needed if each person does what she feels like doing when she feels like doing it. And that may work when you don't have the pressures of pregnancy and, later, parenthood. But that time is over, and now you have the added physical demands of pregnancy in the form of added responsibility, exhaustion and time needed off your feet. You can expect this to bring a definite shift in the current rhythm of your domestic life. Depending on your pregnancy, this could be as dramatic as your being prescribed complete bedrest and being of no help at all with domestic chores, to something as subtle as switching who changes the cat litter through pregnancy, as this activity is dangerous to your unborn baby.

Besides keeping the chaos and bad feelings at bay, taking time to consciously decide who is responsible for the various household chores will clarify what you each want in the way of care for your home life and at the same time give you permission to kick back and do a little relaxing when you know your personal responsibilities around the house are completed.

Divvying Up Your Domestic Duties

Now there is nothing tricky about this shifting of household responsibilities; you just rearrange who is doing what and go forward. The challenge comes in noticing that this reassignment needs to take place, talking with one another about this change and making a decision together about how your domestic tasks will be done differently. Here are some pointers to ensure this is just as easy as it looks for you and your partner.

➤ Write down what you are both agreeing to on the following list or on your own piece of paper. Then double check with each other as you are going along or at the end of your conversation to ensure you have both decided on the same things.

➤ Be specific when making your list. If you are volunteering to cook meals, which meals are you volunteering for? All of them, just dinners, just dinners on the weekends? Clarify exactly to what you are agreeing. This will lessen the chance for misunderstandings down the road.

➤ Set up your initial plan as a test. See how realistic your domestic commitments are. You will likely have to do some tweaking once you begin. That is to be expected.

➤ Pay attention to when the demands of the pregnancy begin to affect you or your partner's ability to complete some of the tasks. When this happens, look for ways that others can take on some added responsibilities, or simplify the household duties. You could do this by lowering your standards for a while, cutting out the extras, asking friends and family for assistance, or hiring some help.

➤ Make this conversation on cleanup a fun one. Get some great food to eat, go to a setting you both love or play some fun music. Make it a nice interaction between the two of you. If you can find no pleasure in the thought of sitting down with your mate and assigning household chores, look at the activity from a bigger perspective. In pregnancy, you are building a new life together. See planning the care of your home life as a necessary foundation from which to begin.

➤ Start the process by each of you going through the list and choosing the tasks that sound the most fun. When doing this, build on your interests and look to take on those things you like or are good at.

So, roll up your sleeves and dive in.

HOUSEHOLD TASKS: WHO IS RESPONSIBLE FOR WHAT, WHEN AND HOW OFTEN?

Clean the bathrooms

Take out the trash and recycling

Wash the dishes

The care of and clean up after the family pets

Cook meals

Pay the bills

Do the laundry

Vacuum and dust

Outdoor jobs like mowing and shoveling

Other:

Other:

Other:

Once the baby is born, your household responsibilities will go through another big shift. A whole new set of chores related to caring for your baby will be added to the list, and your schedule will look nothing like it does now. The key in all of this is to stay open and flexible. Don't see any one chore as yours for eternity. Take responsibility for it while it works, and do something different when it stops working. You may even want to consider going through this process again after you have comfortably transitioned to life with your baby, or sooner if you notice a dark cloud of frustration, chaos or resentment forming around your domestic life.

Interdependence

You thought you were stepping into interdependence, a life of being yourself and joined to another all at the same time, when you said, "I do" at the altar. But that was nothing compared to saying, "We're having a baby." Now, joint decision making and accepting the quirks of the other takes on a whole new meaning. The routine is no longer about each of you doing whatever you want whenever you want. Your baby links you to one another in a whole new way.

At some point in your pregnancy, it is likely you will feel panic in your early awareness of this reality. A pregnant woman can suddenly realize, "I really need my spouse to help take care of me now." This challenge to your sense of personal safety can be a very vulnerable feeling especially if you are used to being very independent. It can be initially uncomfortable, but it is a normal part of moving into interdependence with one another.

Wherever you are in the process of building interdependence, the two of you get to decide together what you want. What do you want interdependence to look like within your relationship? How can you move from your prepregnant lives to the pregnant one in which you both now find yourselves? Strengthening your ability to

operate as a couple from a position of interdependence will have a huge impact on your ability to work well through your pregnancy and into parenthood.

So, let's go straight to the bottom line: what does healthy interdependence look like? Based upon the details of your cultural heritage, your personal outlook, the demands of your job and other personal factors, interdependence will look a bit different for every couple. Given that, here are some key attributes of interdependence. Keep them in mind as this new dynamic begins to take shape within your relationship.

➤ You make decisions together. This doesn't mean it's always easy, but you both have a voice, and one is not railroading the other in the process.

➤ You rely on each other and, at the same time, you still rely on yourself.

➤ You sometimes wish you could just do it all your way. For once in your life, you wouldn't have to deal with the desires of this other person.

➤ Instead of two different lifestyles coexisting, you begin to
develop a combined lifestyle within your relationship that
is uniquely your own. This is the way you get things done,
how you spend evenings or your rituals at the dinner table.
This lifestyle will become so much a part of you, that, at a
point, you will not even notice it any longer. It has become
your normal rhythm of life. You only see it when someone
from the outside comments on how different or unique it is.

It is likely that you and your partner have already had some
experience that pulled you into interdependency with each other.
This could have been in the planning and preparation of your
wedding, in the decisions you made about where you live, the ways
you work together to manage your household or in the process you
went through to decide to have a baby.

One place in your pregnancy where you will find a dramatic
example of interdependency is in your preparations for labor. If you
are planning to have your baby with both of you in the delivery
room, you need each other. You need to work together to plan what
to bring, strategies for managing pain, and how you will involve
other family members. Sara and her partner ran headlong into the
challenges of true interdependence about this very issue.

*At about twenty weeks in our pregnancy, my husband and I
were driving home from a friend's house, and I began telling him
some of my concerns about labor and how much I needed him to
be strong and present for me during that time. I needed him to
reassure me that he was up for the challenge. I wanted to know that
he would be there, fully committed to assist me with this overwhelming challenge. But, instead ,he suggested getting a labor
coach just for himself to help him be the best labor coach he could
for me. Now, this is an innocent enough statement from an
unknowing and perfectionist father-to-be, but given the state of
mind I was in when he said it, I lost it!*

*What in the world was he talking about, a special coach for
him — who does he think is doing the bulk of the work here? So,
I tried to give him an out, "Honey, let's get a special coach that can
work with both of us."*

"No," he said, "I want her to work just with me and then I

can work with you. "

I need the attention on me, not on my husband. And he is sitting over there thinking he needs some kind of special support and attention? What about me? I'm the one birthing a baby.

Suddenly, all of the images of him and me working together to get this baby out of me were shattered. I saw him as needy and wanting support while I was strapped with the most challenging physical experience of my life. Who would support me? I really needed him now and the nature of his own needs left me feeling all alone with this growing baby inside of me.

Don't be surprised if, in your plans for labor or any other important part of your pregnancy, you find yourself, like Sara, feeling alone, angry or isolated from your partner. Interdependence does not mean you always enjoy the actions of your spouse. In fact, because you have to work so much more closely with one another, it can mean an increase in issue-related conflict or a more direct clash of personal needs. When you find yourselves in this kind of a place:

➤ Take a break and each of you reconsider what is most important in the situation.

➤ Call a good friend to talk through the issue. In this conversation, focus on getting to the heart of what you want as well as clarifying how you can best meet these wants. Choose someone who will help you take responsibility for yourself and steer you clear of blame or shame.

➤ Don't turn a conversation on this topic into a session of partner bashing. If you fall into that trap, you are no better after the conversation. In fact, you may feel even a bit worse.

➤ Take some time to get clear on what you want from your partner.

➤ Verbally commit to each other that you will do what it takes to ensure you both get what you need. These words can make a big difference.

➤ Agree to put in the time required to resolve the issue.

When you are called to work interdependently, as pregnancy demands, there is no doubt it can be challenging. Be patient with each other.

TEST THE INTERDEPENDENCE IN YOUR RELATIONSHIP

Take a moment to test out how you handle six different

dimensions of interdependence. Use this informal quiz as a way to gain some insight into how you are currently reacting to the force of interdependence on your relationship. For each dimension, read the brief description and complete the activity that goes with it.

Dimension One: Standing Up for What Matters Most. Pushover is not a part of interdependency language, so make two lists. The first, how many times in the last month can you recall giving in to your spouse on something that mattered to you? The second, how many times can you recall standing up for what you wanted with your spouse and getting it? If the number of times you have compromised on those really important things is more than the number of times you have gotten what you wanted, it is time to take a stand for yourself.

Dimension Two: Making Joint Decisions. Big or small, it doesn't matter, list out the decisions you have made together with your partner in the last two or three weeks. These are not the decisions you made and reported back on. These are the ones you discussed back and forth, looked over pro and con list for, or shared your respective feelings on until you reached a decision with which you could both live. If you cannot come up with more than three, you are operating more independently than you may really want to be at this point in life. Given the fact that you are about to birth a baby together and will soon face all of the joint decisions this baby will require, you may want to begin strengthening your abilities in this area.

Dimension Three: Making Room for Your Partner. Inter dependency requires that the relationship makes room for the quirks and foibles of both parties. Each partner must step to the side at times and make room for the other. List all of the things your partner wants that you do not want. Of these, how many have you accepted as an inevitable part of your life and how many are you still fighting? If fifty percent or more of your partner's desires are still being fought over, you need to move aside and make some room. You do this by recognizing your partner has needs and wants that are different from yours. You choose to stop fighting about all of these issues and accept more of them as a part of the whole package. Finally, you could even go so far as let your partner's interests in some areas rub off on you. If you stopped fighting them and entertained the idea of giving them a try, you may find some redeeming value in a few of these previously irritating preferences. Let your partner be a positive influence on you in this way.

Dimension Four: Finding Your Balancing Point. Every couple's version of interdependency looks a little bit different. Some are more independently oriented and others are more dependently oriented. The right balance is what works best for you and your partner, what allows both of you to feel peace of mind about how you make decisions and support one another within your relationship.

Use each other's perceptions as means to measure interdependency's critical balance between complete independence on one end of the scale and complete dependence on the other. Your perceptions on this balance may not be one hundred percent accurate, but they will likely be in the ballpark.

To accomplish this, sit down together and give one another very honest answers to the following questions: First, does either of you feel like you are carrying too much responsibility for the other right now? Does either of you feel burdened by some of the other's needs, wants or personal challenges? If the answer is yes to one or more of these questions, it is time to make a shift along the interdependency scale away from dependency and towards independence. Talk a bit about making this kind of a mental shift and see if this is a move required of both or only one of you.

Next, consider if you are living too far on the side of independence. Does either of you feel like you cannot get any time with the other? Do you feel removed from the daily life or thoughts of the other? Do you miss him or her? If the answer is yes to any of these questions, it is time to make a shift away from independence towards dependence on the interdependency scale. Again talk about the concrete outcomes of this kind of shift and decide who needs to do what kind of shifting.

Dimension Five: Stop Agonizing Over the Small Stuff. Given the dynamics of your relationship, write down all the little details of life you wish you could just handle without having to coordinate schedules or debate the correct procedures. Believe it or not, couples haggle over such mundane decisions as methods of loading the dishwasher, how you change the toilet paper roll or the number of different drinking glasses to be used in any one day. Write your own list of these silly, but annoying, bones of contention. If you find your list consisits of more than five disputes over these annoying, insignificant details, you and your partner need to back off a bit and give each other some room to just handle some of the minutia of life without turning all decisions into major negotiations.

Dimension Six: Walking the Precarious Edge of Trust. Finally, interdependence requires a new level of trust. The fact that you are in a committed partnership with one another signals you basically trust each other, but in interdependence, the trust takes on a different orientation. It is less about trusting your partner to love and care for you. You know he loves you, but now you are moving towards trusting that he can and will look out for your best interests in the day-to-day actions and decisions of life. Some factors that can erode this kind of trust are:

➤ Miscommunications due to a lack of attention.

➤ Dropping the ball and not following a responsibility through to completion.

➤ Broken promises.

➤ Committing to something you knew your partner wouldn't really want.

➤ Committing to something without checking with your partner first.

To get a measure on the current state of the trust between the two of you, rate your partner using a ten point scale for each of the five factors that can erode trust listed above.

A score of:

10 Unquestioned trust; trust is never a concern.

5 Means a toss up, half the time trust works and half the time it doesn't.

1 Means having no trust in this area at all. This erosion of trust is constantly present in your life together.

Once you have completed your rating, sit down and talk about the biggest violators of this necessary trust. See what you can uncover that will allow you to begin building support in those areas that are lacking.

Interdependence, like so many other things, is an aspect of life that will be in perpetual motion. You will slide up and down the interdependency scale depending upon all of the different circumstances affecting your life. But with the awareness you now have, you can make many of the necessary course corrections to be sure your interdependency is serving both of you.

When you put it all together, the best part of interdependency is that it allows you to build a beautiful connection with your partner and, through this, there is a comforting bond of intimacy like no other. Even though it can be a challenge, interdependency is well worth the effort.

Pregnant Love

For many couples pregnancy ultimately causes a wonderful deepening in their relationship; you have experienced the miracle of life together. Parts of each of you have combined to create your new and fascinating baby. For many, this tightens the bond that joins you, augmenting the love in your relationship. On the flip side, all

of the stress that comes with it can tear you apart, fraying and picking at any weak spots in your love life. For most, the question is not if your pregnancy will affect the love you have with your partner but how it will be affected.

A TASTE OF THAT FALLING-IN-LOVE MAGIC

There is something about a couple expecting a baby, especially a first baby, that brings some extra zip back into a relationship. You are on the brink of something monumental together; and this energy can be as exhilarating and magical as seeing each other for the first time from across a crowded room. Mary describes how she and her partner enjoyed a time of magic in their pregnancy.

I don't know if this is a normal part of many people's pregnancy experience or not, but I feel like my husband and I are in a stage of falling in love with each other again. Our relationship has that wonderful, excited quality of new lovers. We are so thoughtful and loving to each other and catch ourselves making eyes at one another across crowded rooms. It's like we have a secret nobody else knows about. I am thirty-two weeks along, and this lovely time has been going on for at least a month. There is something very romantic about getting ready to have our first child.

Like the experience of being a newlywed, I know this blissfully romantic time of expecting our baby and being completely in love will also end, but it is so sweet while it lasts. I hope when it does end, my husband and I can come to the other side with a stronger, deeper relationship and love for each other.

Through your pregnancy, this falling-in-love feeling may quietly come and envelop your relationship one day. But that is not the case for all couples. Here are some steps you could consider taking to encourage its presence in your relationship:

➤ Pause the business of your life and take in the magnitude of what you and your partner are really doing together. Think about how amazing it is that the two of you have committed to creating another person together. Allow yourselves the luxury of soaking up the full power of this mind-blowing reality.

➤ Take time each day to really notice your partner. Remember how attractive this person was to you when you first met? Remember all of the things about him that were so interesting? These attributes are still there, so take some time to enjoy them.

➤ Notice where you are being overly critical of your partner and stop. Nobody can feel loving if she is being criticized much of the time. If eighty to ninety percent of what your partner does is "right," let the remaining ten to twenty percent go and watch how much more love the two of you can have.

➤ If your partner is not meeting one of your core needs, instead of coming at him with a sideways slam, sit down and talk directly and respectfully about what you want. Ask questions such as "What do you want when it comes to this issue?" "What is getting in the way of doing what I have asked?" or "What can I do to make it easier to follow up on what is important to me?"

➤ Think about the different ways you are together — physically, mentally, emotionally — and then find time to spend together every day. This could be an extended hug in the morning; curling up together to watch a movie; a long, leisurely phone call; sitting together on the couch with coffee and the Sunday paper; or playing together at your favorite mental pursuit.

➤ Decide to do some things throughout the pregnancy to make your partner feel special. It doesn't need to be a big deal. It could be a card, a special phone call or a note from your unborn baby.

You cannot force that loving feeling, but you sure can do a lot to set the stage for its arrival.

IS STRESS TEARING AT THE FABRIC OF YOUR LOVE?

The downside is that pregnancy can also include times of falling out of love with one another. All of the stress of the pregnancy can take a real toll if you are not careful. Some things you can do to reduce this negative impact are to:

➤ Communicate what is going on inside of you. Even if it feels hard to say, find a loving way to get it across. These negative feelings are real whether you say them or not. Ultimately, it will be much more beneficial for you and your relationship if you get them on the table where you can deal with them directly.

➤ Respect each other's emotional reactions, even if you think they are stress- or hormone-based. Yes, pregnant women can act overly emotional and expectant fathers/partners can be very stressed out, but, at the moment, the reaction they are having is their reality. To discount that reality only makes it worse. Oftentimes, once they feel their reality has been heard and understood, they can see things from a different perspective.

➤ Take some of the challenges or conflicts between each other with a grain of salt. Forgive, forget and move on. This is a time to be careful of not making too much out of a small overreaction.

Throughout the whole nine months, do what you can to keep the pregnancy-related stress on one side of the conflict and the two of you together and unified on the other. When this seems hard to do and you want to begin blaming the other person for the stress you feel, remind yourself you partner is doing the best he can in the situation, that there are so many factors beyond the control of both of you, and that, ultimately, you both want the same things: a healthy baby in your life together. You need each other too much right now to allow stress to get in the way.

An added force of negative stress that could be acting on your relationship is the fear of this pregnancy or your fast-arriving baby impairing or even ruining your relationship. Some common variations of these fears are:

> The demands of caring for your baby could create an irreparable rift in the relationship.
> Your partner might have interest more in the baby than in you.
> Your partner might not find you attractive now that you are a mother or a father to this baby.
> You and your partner could begin to have very different levels of interest in sexual intimacy.
> Your partner may fall out of love with you through all of this.

If you realize you are stressed by one of these, or another related fear about the future of your relationship, it is time to talk with your partner about it. Tell your spouse about the concerns you are having, find out how he is feeling about these concerns, and talk about ways you can address these fears together. It is really important you stop worrying alone and take some positive action to address the situation. After the two of you have had an open conversation, for added support, you could also consider:

> Talking with some close friends who have children and see how they handled similar fears for their own relationship.
> Finding a counselor or coach who can speak to this issue and who you feel moves you in a positive direction.
> Researching it on the Internet to see what you can learn.
> Posting a question on some of the pregnancy websites or chat rooms. You can find some of these sites in the resource

section of the introductory chapter.

➤ Trying to come to this fear or challenging situation from a totally different perspective with your partner. For example, if you are fearful about having different interests in sex, try to create a whole new rhythm for your sex life. Look at sex from the perspective of sensuality, doing only what feels good to both of you or as just one piece of the intimacy pie.

If allowed to run freely, fear will just grow and fester, often causing the exact outcome you were dreading. Don't do anything that could attract all of this negative energy. Take some action so you can mentally let go of it and move on.

PREGNANT SEX

Speaking of sex, as you have probably already found, sex during pregnancy changes a lot! If you don't feel you have enough of the hot-and-bothered details on this topic, pick up a copy of the *Girlfriends Guide to Pregnancy* by Vicki Iovine. This resource does a great job of spelling out exactly — I mean exactly what the physical experience of pregnant sex is all about. Check it out and then get creative to design a sex life that works for your unique relationship. Think about:

➤ Trying different positions, times of day or settings.

➤ Skipping some parts or adding something new.

➤ Listening to and respecting your changing sexual desires and limitations.

➤ Telling your partner about these changes and what you now want from your sex life together.

However you decide to navigate through the physical act of sex, the goal is that you and your partner keep your sexual life alive at some level throughout the pregnancy and on into the completely exhausting phase of life with a new baby. For some relationships, that is no problem and sex is better than ever. But for many others, sex becomes the last thing on one, and sometimes both people's, minds. There are many dimensions that make up a relationship, and a healthy union between two people usually includes some type of sexual spark. This doesn't mean you should expect a daily roll in the hay, but, at the same time, you cannot keep your relationship in balance without some nuances of sexual intimacy showing up here or there.

This intimacy can be found in many ways besides the physical act of sexual relations. Try such things as hand, foot or back massages; a romantic dinner for two with candles and soft music; surprises for each other; lounging in bed together or doing some physical playing together such as frolicking in a swimming pool or lying side by side in the grass. Shoot for making intimate connections the focus of pregnant sex and, although it may not be what you're used to, it will feel good on many levels and neither of you will be disappointed.

LOVING THE EMERGING PARENT IN YOUR PARTNER

Your lover is taking on a new role and so are you. You are each turning into a parent. There is a whole new aspect of this person you can love. Polly relished finding this in her own husband.

Dads are amazing! Watching the dad come out in the man I love is such a wonderful process. We are fifteen weeks along, and he is beginning to get excited about becoming a father. I came back from walking the dog this morning and he had just read an article about the positive effects of a father's presence early on in a baby's life and things fathers can do to be more involved with their children.

It has been fun to watch my husband begin to build his own connections to our baby. He is talking about bringing the baby to me for midnight feedings, taking the baby on afternoon walks and giving the baby her evening bath. I think he is getting excited about becoming a dad. It makes me love him even more.

Tim also found himself wanting to celebrate this new part of his partner and lover.

Last Sunday was Mother's Day. How wonderful it was to celebrate Mother's Day with my partner who will become a mother any day now. We are due tomorrow. It felt really good to recognize her as our unborn baby's mother and acknowledge all of the wonderful motherly qualities I can already see her taking on. She is so nurturing. She is always aware of how her actions will affect the baby. And she has this wonderful new gentleness. I love it!

The rest of the world seemed to take a moment to stop and honor her on the verge of motherhood. She received several phone calls from friends wishing her a happy Mother's Day. She also received several Mother's Day cards in the mail. It is going to be fun to watch this woman I love evolve and find her way as a mother to our baby. I am sure I will learn new things about who she is and what is important to her.

Where is that mom or dad beginning to materialize in your partner? What new parts do you find endearing? What could you do to let your partner know how much you love this new part? You don't need to wait for Mother's or Father's Day to let your spouse know you are proud of the parent he is becoming.

And, as with everything in relationships, the opposite can often be true, and the experience of watching the parent develop within your partner can be far from heartwarming and lead to some really unsettled feelings. Your partner may not respond as you've always known him to, you may find yourself feeling more constrained and inhibited around him, you may feel your spouse has become overly responsible or a host of other normal reactions to this major change taking place within him.

Adding parent into the mix of roles you both play in your relationship is a huge and significant transition in the dynamics of your life together. It makes sense that it could feel a bit uncomfortable. And, as with most concerns you face, the best thing you can do is the simple act of talking with each other about it. Tell each other what is not working and commit to pursue a resolution that allows you both to feel comfortable and peaceful with the changes in your relationship.

Summary

Set Your Expectations Straight

It Will Ultimately Help Your Relationship if You:
- Ask for what you want from both your relationship and your partner.
- Listen to what you partner is trying to tell you.
- Acknowledge with one another the changes taking place within your relationship.
- Look for opportunities to build a healthy interdependency with one another.
- Put the necessary time into addressing any conflicts that may be causing a rift in your relationship.

It Will Ultimately Hurt Your Relationship if You:
- Maintain unrealistic expectations of your partner or your relationship.
- Expect your partner to be capable of meeting all of your needs.
- Avoid discussing the tough issues.
- Cave in on things that really matter to you.
- Take too much personal responsibility for the challenges before you and your spouse.
- Discount your own feelings, reactions, wants or desires as you go through the transitions of your pregnancy.

Resources

On Relationships

The Relationship Cure: A Five-Step Guide for Building Better Connections with Family, Friends and Lovers, John M. Gottman and Joan Declaire. (New York, NY: Crown Publishing, 2001.)

I Only Say This Because I Love You: How the Way We Talk Can Make or Break Family Relationships Throughout Our Lives, Deborah Tannen. (New York, NY: Random House, 2001.)

The Seven Principles For Making Marriage Work, John Gottman and Nan Silver. (New York, NY: Three Rivers Press, 2000.)

The Good Marriage: How And Why Love Lasts, Judith Wallerstein and Sandra Blakeslee. (New York, NY: Warner Books, 1996.)

Why Marriages Succeed or Fail, And How You Can Make Yours Last, John M. Gottman and Nan Silver. (Fireside, 1995.)

That's Not What I Meant: How Conversational Style Makes or Breaks Relationships, Deborah Tannen. (New York, NY: Ballantine Books, 1991.)

On Sex

The Mother's Guide to Sex: Enjoying Your Sexuality Through All Stages of Motherhood, Anne Semans and Cathy Winks. (Three Rivers Press, 2001.)

Passionate Marriage: Love, Sex and Intimacy in Emotional Committed Relationships, David Schnarch. (New York, NY: Henry Holt, 1998.)

The Girlfriend's Guide to Pregnancy: Or Everything Your Doctor Won't Tell You, Vicki Iovine. (New York, NY Pocket Books, 1998.)

STRATEGY NINE
LIGHTEN YOUR LOAD BY FACING YOUR PREGNANCY LOSSES

The potential losses associated with pregnancy can come in all forms, some big and dramatic and others subtle and hard to find. Whatever its size, loss and the sadness that goes with it during this time which is supposed to be so joyous is especially out of place and confusing.

What is it that has you reading this strategy on loss at this point in your pregnancy? Take a moment to get really clear on what is calling you to explore this painful topic.

Are you in the throws of your own pregnancy loss? Are you looking for some help and a place to be understood? Do you want to know you are not alone? You may want some reassurance that the intensity of your emotions or reactions are very normal. Are you hoping to find some comfort or peace of mind to unlock a little of your pain?

Are you feeling an edge of sadness and hoping to help yourself understand why? You may be experiencing a loss you have not allowed yourself to acknowledge. This may be the right time to remove any criticism about what feelings or losses are permissible.

Are you feeling caught in the fear of all the possible losses you could experience in pregnancy? If so, it can be helpful to see that others have made it through your worst nightmares and are still in one piece. They will never forget, but, emotionally they are able to continue. They are able to live rich and happy lives, and so can you, no matter what might happen to you or your baby in this pregnancy.

Or, instead, is your interest grounded in a desire to understand what it is really like to go through a loss associated with pregnancy?

You may have a friend or family member who has or is going through some kind of a loss. You may want to know how you can provide them with some added support. You may want to open up your heart and have some compassion for a loss you just don't understand.

By getting very clear on what has brought you to these pages, you will be able to make the most of what you find within them.

Below is a collection of stories, each on a different loss in pregnancy. These stories can be hard to read and, at the same time, they cut to the heart of what such a loss really feels like. Furthermore, they show you a pathway through, which could provide some light if you are facing a particularly dark time in a similar loss. Don't feel you need to read all of these stories, take what will help you along in your journey and leave the rest.

Unplanned Pregnancy

Wanda thought she was long past having children when she became pregnant again.

'I am forty-two, a busy mom of two, and now fifteen weeks pregnant with a third child. This must be someone else's life, it cannot be mine. How am I going to manage the needs of my two children plus a baby?

Telling Nathan, my ten-year-old son, and Brita, my twelve-year-old daughter was the absolute hardest part. Trying to explain

to them why I am pregnant was ten times worse than any fear I have about the actual pregnancy. They both just stared at us in total disbelief. I could tell exactly what they were thinking, how could their mom and dad do this to them? It has been several weeks since we first talked about it, and they seem to be warming up to the idea. Last night, they were actually talking about who would get to be the first to babysit.

I thought about an abortion, but I really believe I need to take responsibility for my actions, and an abortion just seemed like an easy way out. I am not a young girl who is unprepared to become a parent. I am an adult in a family who can care for the children I bring into this world. Plus, I was pretty sure that I'd have regrets if I went ahead with an abortion.

With those two challenges sorted out, now my concerns are beginning to turn to my baby. I'm no spring chicken, and I know all of the risk factors increase having a baby at my age. But, I can tell I am already falling in love with this child, and I want to protect it and keep it healthy. I should probably be more concerned about how I will physically make it through labor, but I cannot even think about that right now. I need to just continue taking this one day at a time.

This is not the life I thought I'd be living right now. I am sad that I will not be as carefree with my two older children for a while. A new baby is really going to slow me down. I am sad that the next couple of years with my kids will not be the way I imagined them to be. By having this baby, I feel like we'll miss out on some special times we could have had together. The ultimate irony of all of this is that the night of conception was our fifteenth wedding anniversary. We'd spent dinner talking about all of the things we could begin doing now that the kids were getting older. I guess the midwife wasn't kidding when she told me the antibiotics I was taking could affect the functioning of my birth-control pill.

An unplanned pregnancy is one of those events that spins your life in a whole new direction. If you are committed to carrying and then raising a baby you did not plan for, let these thoughts aid you in stepping into your new life with this child:

➤ This commitment to keep your baby is an option. You have choices and you need to consider them all so you are completely clear on the fact that you chose to raise this baby to adulthood.

➤ You have nine months to get prepared and mentally alter your life plan; don't get overwhelmed by deciding you need to have it all set up in the next week.

➤ You can have a baby and still do the few things that matter most to you.

> The baby will likely sleep a lot the first three to four months, unless they are overly fussy or colicky, so use the sleeping time you have in these early months to take care of yourself and attend to those things that are most important.

> Infants are quite portable. Take your new baby along with you.

> When you feel the squeeze of losing your personal time to this baby, remind yourself that infancy and toddlerhood go by so fast and these early years are filled with so much love, it would be a shame to let other parts of your life rush you through this beautiful time. Then, watch for the times when your baby needs less from you, like when he is sleeping or engrossed in an activity of his own and, instead of doing the dishes, choose to do something that gives back to you.

> Life is long and this baby will be in school in five years. You may move at a slower pace during these first five years, still doing what is important to you, just not as much of it. Once the baby is in school, you can pick up the pace.

> Ask for what you want from employers, parents, your spouse, friends and childcare providers. You'd be surprised how often you can get your needs met, even in an area to which you thought they'd never agree.

Don't give up more than you are comfortable with and never let yourself become a victim to this pregnancy.

Miscarriage

At ten weeks along in her pregnancy, Dee had a miscarriage.

Miscarriages are strange. To me, it was the death of someone that wasn't ever fully here and at the same time someone who was a part of every second of my life. This made it a bizarre grieving process for my husband and me. But maybe all grieving processes feel bizarre; they hurt, feel awkward and are rarely understood by those who have not experienced the same intensity of pain. But still, somehow miscarriages feel different than a postbirth death. Life is incredibly changed and yet the day-to-day living has not changed at all. There were no physical signs of this baby. I had no big bulbous stomach. We hadn't felt him or her move yet. I knew nothing about who this person was. But, at the same time, we were beginning to build a relationship with this child. All we had to do to end any connection this baby had with us or the rest of the world was to cancel our baby errands and stop cleaning out that extra room for the nursery. That was it. Life over.

But, mentally, our transition was just beginning. I couldn't let go so quickly or so easily. I felt incredible pain and sorrow and loss. I had spent ten weeks beginning to prepare for this baby and it was going to take me some time to let go of this little life.

I found my own body to be a wonderful metaphor for this process of letting go. The blood of a pregnant woman begins to carry extra hormones during the pregnancy. They build up slowly throughout the first trimester and, if the pregnancy ends in a miscarriage, these hormones slowly decrease. My miscarriage was the result of an ectopic pregnancy, so I had these hormone levels checked at least ten times over the month following our miscarriage. I watched them slowly work their way back down to prepregnant levels. Just like the hormones in my body, it took me some time to get used to the reality of suddenly not being pregnant.

Our miscarriage happened in the middle of the night, and I can remember waking up the next morning at dawn and walking my now-empty body down stairs. I lay down on the living room floor in helpless defeat and cried. Everything had changed in the span of a couple hours, and I was alone. Our baby, who was an invisible, but very present part of our lives, now would never be here. My sense of the future was gone. Having this miscarriage was the hardest thing my husband and I have had to go through so far in our marriage. We both felt such a sense of loss.

Mixed with the pain and sorrow, as is often the case, we also gained some new insight. First, my husband and I learned that he and I could be there for each other. We learned that we could pull it together, support one another and get through it together. That is an incredible thing to know about your marriage. One memory I have, and will probably never forget, is of my husband and me sitting together in a big overstuffed chair, hugging and crying together. It was the first evening after the miscarriage, and we spent it longing for all that wouldn't be.

The other thing we learned is how important it was for us to talk with people about the loss of this baby. We were so thankful that we hadn't waited the standard three months before we began telling people we were pregnant. We told our family and close friends about our pregnancy right away, and that made it easy to have them there to support us when it so abruptly ended. They had seen our excitement and knew about our new-baby preparations while it was a happy joyous time. Now, with a miscarriage, they understood and could support us in the depth of our sadness.

Prior to the miscarriage I had made plans to spend the weekend cleaning out that extra bedroom and begin its transformation into a nursery. Our miscarriage happened on Thursday night. There was no longer any reason to spend time cleaning out the room. I did it anyway.

If you have had a miscarriage, it can be helpful to hear the spiritual reflections of those women who have experienced this pain before you:

➤ This baby is always spiritually close to my family and me.

➤ I will always feel connected to this baby, and I know the spirit of this baby feels a similar connection to me. This connection will last throughout my lifetime if not longer.

➤ I read a poem about miscarriage and, in the first two lines, I saw an image of this baby as a little four-year-old boy with tousled hair. This is the image I always keep now when I think of my miscarriage, and I will never forget him.

➤ This lost baby made the way ready for my beautiful baby girl to enter the world.

➤ I think of this baby every year on its due date. The date is not written down anywhere. I know I will never forget it.

➤ This baby will always live in my heart and mind.

➤ One day I will be with this baby again, and I will know him and he will know me.

➤ No matter where I go, the spirit of this baby is always with me.

➤ I love this baby, and I know my baby loves me.

These kinds of thoughts tie into your spiritual beliefs and can give you meaning, comfort and connection about a baby whom you have had to let go due to a miscarriage.

Stillborn

The loss of a full-term baby affects everyone whose life it touches, from midwives, doctors, doulas and nurses to family, friends and neighbors. Everyone sees life a little differently after being close to the death of an unborn baby after that critical twenty-eighth week. Jamie was four weeks from delivering her own baby when she went through the stillborn death of her sister's baby.

When she told me, I could feel it like a knife cutting into my heart. Sarah's baby, now three days overdue, had died. They had no answers about why. She and Tom were going to wait for two days to see if her body would naturally begin labor and, if not, she would go in at the end of the second day and be induced.

We went over to their house that night. We all cried and hugged. Our two pregnant bellies seemed to take up all of the extra space in the room. Mine with a kicking baby still waiting to be born and hers with her beloved child already gone before he had even taken his first breath.

Sarah was in shock. She cried a lot and spent most of the night with her arms wrapped around her stomach, cradling her unborn son. Tom was trying hard not to cry. Every time Sarah broke down, he got all choked up. I think that for him, watching Sarah in so much pain was almost as hard as the fact that his son had died.

They told us they wanted to plan a service for the baby, but that night Tom and Sarah just wanted to grieve the loss of what was supposed to be the joyous arrival of their baby. Their whole world had changed within an hour. The life they were moving towards was snatched away with their son, and now they didn't know where they were. Their little son was gone.

They did end up having to be induced, and we went down to the hospital to meet James Michael. He was a beautiful baby with thick brown hair and lovely smooth skin. We took pictures and the nurse cut a lock of his hair and gently placed it in Tom's hand. I cried through the whole thing. I cried for James, that he would never look into the eyes of the wonderful parents waiting for him. I cried for my own unborn baby, knowing that the reality of this is a possibility for everyone, including him. I cried for myself and my husband because we loved our little baby so much and through that love we are so vulnerable to these kinds of tragedies. Most of all I cried for Sarah and Tom. Everything they wanted was gone. Instead of a lifetime, all they had was a handful of hours with this beautiful baby boy.

Tears came out of Sarah's eyes, but she didn't make much of a sound the whole time she was with James. She held him, lovingly stroked his little hands, and adjusted his hair first this way and then that. She just gazed into his face. Her firstborn son. They spent six hours with him. Then Tom took him to the nurse. He would be cremated for the funeral. I will never forget that moment, as James left Sarah's arms. The look on her face, the painful letting go that she had to do.

Now it is three years later. Tom and Sarah are amazing. They have planted a garden for James and keep him alive in their family through pictures, books and the cards they received at the funeral. Sarah wrote a baby book for him and instead of the long lists of firsts, she wrote all about the process of healing, telling James what it was like. They now have a baby girl, Jennifer, and are pregnant with a third child. They are happy and are living a good life. They will never forget James and, at the same time, they have been able to continue living their lives here on earth while James waits for them in another place.

Margaret has delivered two stillborn babies in her career as a midwife. Each time, it had been an experience she would never forget. She is in awe at the strength of the mothers and fathers as they fall headfirst into such a horrific outcome to what was supposed to be the most joyous moments of their birth process. She has a small and humble gift to offer all parents who have had to endure such a loss.

Margaret's gift: Remember that every moment of life is precious from the first heartbeat of your unborn baby to the last breath of your greatest grandparent. You lived the brief months of your baby's precious life together. Through this, you are forever bonded to one another. Hold this beautiful connection close to your heart and let it continue to fill your soul with love until you can be united in some form again.

Birth Defects

Kara's baby was perfect in almost every way.

Samuel James was born two days ago. I am hopelessly in love with him. He is a beautiful, healthy baby boy with a wild head of red hair and the softest fair skin you can imagine. He has a wonderful disposition and, for the most part, is so content. I am so relieved that he is here and doing so well. Our one challenge is nursing. He is doing what is called tongue thrusting, where he sticks his tongue out when he is trying to suck. It really makes nursing hard, but the nurse said this is very common for babies born with Down's Syndrome.

I was forty when I got pregnant with Sam. I already had two children, ages four and two, so I figured I had healthy babies and my age was of no concern. But my husband and I both like to have as much information as we can, so when we were offered a screening test for Down's Syndrome and other genetic problems, we chose to take it.

Well, our score came back very low, indicating there could be a problem. I have this wonderful midwife, and she did her best to reassure me that this result didn't necessarily mean anything was wrong, it just meant we needed to get more information. I left her office feeling cautiously optimistic that my baby was alright.

Our next step was to get a level II ultrasound. I felt my heart sink when the doctor didn't like what she saw. She was fairly certain that our baby had Down's Syndrome. I felt like I wanted to gag. She suggested we get an amniocentesis to confirm it. I began to cry. Two weeks later, the results of the amnio came back and we knew that Sam had Down's Syndrome.

Five years ago, my cousin gave birth a daughter with Down's Syndrome and I watched her incredible love for this little girl. This experience helped me know for certain that I would not terminate my pregnancy, no matter what we found out with all of the tests. I never even had to go through the agony of deciding whether or not to keep the baby.

Now, we begin caring for this beautiful baby. We will have to wait to find out how severe Sam's Down's Syndrome is. Maybe he will be able to live on his own someday and maybe not. Today, our big challenge is teaching him how to nurse. Who knows what it will be in the years to come.

New life is precious and full of hope in whatever form it takes. Your little baby's drive for life is as strong as any other's, even if he doesn't fit our definition of normal. This is true for a baby with Down's Syndrome or the hosts of other challenges that can afflict a baby. Your baby wants to be here, to experience all that his life has to offer.

If you have any doubt of your baby's deepest gratitude for bringing him into this world as is, take a moment to reflect on the pounding of his heart, the kicking of his limbs and the life force that keeps his little body growing and developing. Think about those tiny premature babies who fight against all of the odds to stay alive. Life, in any form, has the potential to be a rich and fulfilling experience.

Your baby is not worrying about physical limitations, concerned about the prejudiced nature of our society or worried that he won't be as smart or as good looking as everybody else. Your baby just wants a chance to enter this new and unbelievable world, to breathe in the gift of life you have to give. It may not be the life you had planned for, but his life will be beautiful for what it is, in whatever form it takes.

Having a Boy When You Wanted a Girl

When Pauline was pregnant with her second child, she really wanted to have a girl, but instead she had her second boy.

Ever since I was a child, I always dreamed of having a little girl. I imagined us going out to lunch and shopping together. I imagined I would teach her all of the things I have learned about how to be a strong woman in a male-oriented world. I looked forward to her wedding, having babies of her own and that incredible bond that can form between mothers and daughters. But now none of that will be in my life. I have two boys. Add my husband and my dog, and I am surrounded by penises.

Obviously, this is not one of life's biggest tragedies, but I really feel the loss of that daughter I will never have. I find myself longing to take care of a little girl. I want to fix her hair, have tea parties together and have people say she looks just like me. I see all of the stores filled with beautiful little spring dresses, and it is depressing to think I will never get to pick one out for my daughter. I have this set of skills I could use with little girls that just don't apply to little boys, things like French-braiding hair, shaving legs and knowing how to have a great week despite the arrival of your period. This all-boy life is not the one I envisioned for myself, and I struggle, trying to see how it will fit me.

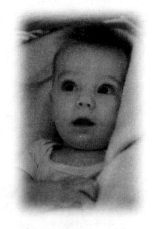

I love my sons to death, and I wouldn't trade them for the world, but they will never quite understand me like my daughter would have. Our world still creates very different lives for most males and females, and my son's, life experiences will just be very different.

It is hard not to have that son or daughter you have longed for. As with any loss, your life will be different than the one you expected. If this is a loss you are facing, address it head on. Don't minimize it or tell yourself it is silly. The feelings you have are real, and it is a sad thing not to have the child you always wanted. Do something to attend to these feelings and then consider what you could do to satisfy the desires you have for a little girl or boy in your life. You could adopt a child, play a special role in the life of a niece or nephew, or volunteer as a mentor to a needy boy or girl.

Pauline has made her loss even larger by making all kinds of assumptions about how sons are and how daughters are. And yes, some of them may be true, but who knows who these little babies will become as they grow up? If you have only boys or all girls and are feeling the loss of never parenting the little girl or boy you have longed for, here are some slightly different perspectives on the whole thing.

> ➤ With every generation, the roles of the sexes becomes more and more open to individual interpretation. Who knows what wonderful things your daughters will accomplish or the intensity of your son's emotions or his ability to be nurturing?

➤ Mothers and daughters can be very close, and they can also fight like cats and dogs and never come to peace with one another. Sons can grow up with a special place in their hearts for mom, or they can cut themselves off and rarely call or visit. The point is to every beautiful dream of how it could be, there is a less-desired reality that could also be waiting in your future. Just because you have dreamed of a wonderful upside doesn't mean that will be the result if you have the boy or girl you are longing for.

➤ One of your boys or girls could choose an alternative lifestyle, and that could result in a whole new picture of adult life with your child.

➤ Many girls like sports and many boys like dance class and reading. If there is something you have longed to do with that little girl or boy you didn't have, try doing it with the girl or boy you do have. Who knows, he may love it.

➤ There is the potential for a special bond between siblings of the same sex. They usually have more in common than siblings of different sexes. Maybe the gift you have given your children is a potential lifelong bond with their brother or sister.

Take these thoughts as a small gift to realign your view on your situation and lighten the load of your loss.

Divorce or an Affair During Your Pregnancy

Ann was halfway through her pregnancy when she found out her boyfriend did not want to marry her and raise their baby together.

At first, I was furious. He had the nerve to come to my house, stand in my kitchen and tell me he loved someone else. He went on and on about how she is the one he wants to marry. I could not believe it. I was so mad ,I just wanted him out of my life.

Now, I am scared. I feel overwhelmed because I was really counting on him to support me through this. He has left me for some other woman. What kind of man would do that to the woman carrying his baby? I think it is so irresponsible and immature that he is choosing not to be a part of this baby's life.

I could tell something was going on. He wasn't spending much time with me, and he was always very distracted those few times he actually was around. I just figured he was having a tough time getting used to the pregnancy. Neither of us had planned on getting pregnant, but I thought we loved each other, and I figured it would all work out in the end.

The last thing I ever wanted was to raise a baby alone. I know my family will help out, and they have been pretty understanding. But I can see the disappointment in their eyes, and I know this is not what they wanted for me. I'm disappointed, too. I feel like both my baby and I will be at such a disadvantage in life.

I am also really hurt. I feel like he didn't pick me as the one to marry because of the pregnancy because I wasn't exciting anymore now that I am pregnant. Because I represented being tied down. He loved me before I was pregnant, at least that is what he told me. Why doesn't he love me now? How can a man leave a woman who is pregnant with his child? Why doesn't he want to be a part of this baby's life?

In my head, I can tell myself this is not about me, that it is all about him. But I am afraid now no man will ever be interested in me, a woman alone with a baby.

Even without a pregnancy, getting through a broken heart can be very tough. You feel like you will never love anyone again. You worry nobody will ever be romantically interested in you. You have to face loneliness and singlehood in a world filled with couples. Then, if you add a pregnancy, you have all of that plus the intense feelings of vulnerability without a committed partner to help you feel secure. You have the powerful feeling of responsibility for providing a good life for your unborn baby. You alone are saddled with a new set of financial responsibilities in caring for yourself and a small child. You have two highly emotional situations piled on top of each other. It can all erode your peace of mind.

But, right now, the best thing you can do for yourself is keep from getting caught in your overwhelming emotions, isolation or the depression both can bring. Some ways to take care of yourself right now are to:

> ➤ Decide what you really want. Do you want to raise the baby yourself? Do you want to put it up for adoption? Do

you want to live with your parents, another family member or an intimate friend and raise your baby with them? You have options. Step back and, given this change of events, decide how you want to proceed.

➤ Call upon your support system to help you. Find people to be an active part of your pregnancy, people with whom you can have some fun, people who will visit you when you're down, people who will help you get involved in some new things, people who can be a part of your baby's life with you, and people who can support and love you no matter what you decide to do in this situation. (Look to the first strategy on building a support system if you don't know how to find these people in your life.)

➤ Acknowledge for yourself that this just plain sucks. Don't be polite or nice about it. Yell and scream, write an unmailable letter you can later destroy, throw darts at his picture or purge him from your life by getting rid of all of the things he has ever given you. Let your anger help you reclaim your own strength.

➤ Then, take advantage of this newfound strength. If you want to keep this baby, you do have what it takes to follow through on your decision. With the help of those who care, you can create a very good life for yourself and your child. Trust this and create a wonderful, positive vision of how good it can be for you and your baby. Then use your perseverance and determination to get what you want and make this vision your reality.

C-Section When You Wanted to Have a Natural Birth

Tony's partner Alicia had a C-section, which resulted in a beautiful baby boy.

When Alicia and I planned for labor, we did everything possible to prepare for a natural birth process. We took special classes, we practiced diligently at home, she took herbal remedies and we reviewed every technique known for relaxing through pain. So, I was not surprised when she was completely distraught over the fact that her thirty-two labor process ended in a five-minute C-section.

What has caught me off guard is how upset she continues to be over the whole thing. She is so angry with herself that she did not birth our baby naturally. She talks about how she has failed in her ability to be strong and follow through on what mattered most to her. She is so angry that she let the hospital staff intervene in her natural process. After twenty-four hours of laboring, they finally convinced her to take a shot of morphine so she could get some rest. She is convinced that is what began her on the path to this C-section, but she was so exhausted, I don't know how she could have done anything else. She is so angry and feels so victimized by the whole experience, I am overwhelmed by it. I don't know how to help her.

It is almost like she doesn't want to let go of it. Here we have this beautiful, healthy baby boy, whom I can see she loves so much. So my thinking says, who cares if the labor didn't end the way we expected. We also didn't expect thrity-two hours of labor, but she is not mad about that. None of the labor was in our control. It just happened. Whenever I try to bring up this point, she gets angry and tells me I don't understand.

As our midwife told us, you just don't know what kind of a labor you might have, so you really need to let go of any expectations you have about how it should be and just keep your eye on the prize, a healthy baby and a healthy mom. In my opinion, we did that. We tried to stay as natural as possible, but we also adjusted as we needed to given all of the unknowns with which we were dealing. But Alicia doesn't see it this way at all. We have had some really big fights because I encouraged her to take the morphine and get some rest. So, in addition to the hospital staff, she is also blaming me for what happened to her. I just wish she would let go and move on with me into our new life with our baby.

If this sounds at all like your story, stop beating up yourself and your body over your perception of an unacceptable performance in labor. There is no such thing. Labor is not an Olympic sport, and there are no points for style. The goal is just to allow your body to do its thing and, if needed, give it some added help to ensure the end result is a healthy mom and a healthy baby. In this, there is no room for predetermined expectations. No matter what happened in your labor, you did your personal best. It is time to set aside your beliefs about how you think it is supposed to be or your anger about what happened and focus on your own health and that of your baby. That is what really matters in all this.

An Unhealthy Pregnancy Instead of the One You Dreamed of

Aya did not have a dream pregnancy, in fact, they were probably the longest nine months of her entire life.

I am working very hard to keep a positive attitude, but I am twenty-six weeks along, and I have been sick the whole time. Last night, for example, my husband and I went out to the movies. On the way home, I had to stop him so I could get out of the car and throw up. Feeling this bad for so long has really affected every part of my life. I have no motivation and, at this point, I can barely do my job, I haven't seen a friend in weeks, and just going to the post office is a big deal. Whatever I do, I feel miserable the whole time. I really cannot remember what it is like to feel healthy, alive and vibrant. It is so ironic. Here I am growing new life inside of me, and I feel half-dead.

I never dreamed that pregnancy would be like this for me. I always thought I would love being pregnant, that I would be so happy when I was pregnant. It is just the opposite, I am the most sad and worn-out person I have ever been. I am no fun to be around. I just want to lie on the couch all day. Even the simple act of making conversation with someone is often too much work. I know I am feeling depressed. I'm just not sure how much of this depression is the sick feeling and how much is my emotional state. I am trying to make the best of it, reminding myself to be thankful I am pregnant and that we have a healthy baby. But I can tell you, at times, it is very hard to be thankful about anything! My husband and I went into all of this thinking we wanted two children, but at this point, I don't think I can stomach another one.

You may be living through the strains of a totally unpleasant pregnancy. And, like some, you are coping just fine with it. You are not feeling any great emotional loss. It is clearly no fun, but you don't feel like something is missing or you have lost something very important to you. Be thankful if this is your reaction.

However, for others, this same kind of an experience leads to a truly painful feeling of loss on top of all the physical unplesantness. These people have found themselves in a pregnancy totally different from what they expected or wanted for themselves.

If the latter is the case for you, take some time to understand what you feel you have lost, then look for small tidbits of it in the pregnancy you have. Finally, make an effort to plan some event or find something small each day that you can use to buoy your spirits. This could be:

> Visiting a special friend.

> Spending as much time as possible in a location where you feel the best you can, maybe the shower, a place where it is cool and dark, your own bed, a swimming pool or resting outside.

> Taking a couple of minutes to watch something small and simple from nature — for example, the falling rain, a spring flower, even an ant struggling to move a pebble. These kinds of things can take you outside yourself for a bit and remind you of how amazing life really is, even in your very compromised state.

> Mentally removing yourself from your challenged body for a bit of time. Try different things to see if you can separate yourself from your body and if this mental separation can give you some relief. Some things to try are picking an object outside of your window and focusing on being in that object. It could be a tree, a car, a swing or a hammock. Pick anything that appeals to you. Then, imagine yourself sitting in that object. Get all of your senses involved in this mental journey; feel it, smell it, hear it and see it from this new perspective. If that doesn't work, try losing yourself in movies or books on tape. Watch or listen to as many as you can stand. Put all of your concentration into the story and see if you can, for a bit, forget about the unpleasant times you are facing in your pregnancy.

When you are feeling unhealthy or are physically challenged, it is vital that you put your focus on just getting through one day at a time. Whatever discomforts are accompanying your pregnancy, remember the days you have to live with them are limited and, although it may seem a long way off, it will end eventually.

Strategies for Living Through A Pregnancy Loss

No matter what specific situation you face, a pregnancy-related loss just plain hurts. Let the six reflections below guide you along through your journey with grief and out the other side of its dark shadow.

REFLECTION ONE: FIND SOME PEOPLE WHO UNDERSTAND YOUR LOSS

You are in the throes of a very tough situation. It is really painful. The last thing you need are people's bizarre reactions making it harder. But whether you're up for it or not, here they are. Every day, you have to interact with someone who doesn't know what to say to you or how to deal with this situation you're living through. They say something like:

➤ "My sister-in-law never really recovered from this exact experience," bringing even more doom and gloom into your world.

➤ "Oh well, you'll be over it soon," minimizing the struggles you are having.

➤ "It's all a part of God's plan." This one is tricky because, yes, your loss could be a part of a larger plan and seeing it that way can be a useful perspective to take, but when someone lays it on in the midst of your pain, it can feel less than helpful. This kind of a realization is one you want to get to in your own way and at your own pace.

➤ This is one of the worst reactions you may receive. They say nothing at all to acknowledge your loss. They avoid the topic at all costs and leave a gigantic white elephant sitting smack in the middle of your relationship. It can leave you feeling isolated, cut off and alone with your pain.

Unfortunately, none of the people making these comments understands what it means to be going through this experience, or, if they do share a similar loss, they have forgotten what is really helpful. They may be uncomfortable, confused or afraid of their own pain and are unable to reach out to you. Or, they may be trying to reach out, and they just aren't doing it in a way that works very well for you. This doesn't mean they are bad people; they are likely doing the best they know how to for you right now.

This is a time to get really intentional about with whom you will spend your time. Who do you know that gets it? These are the people that:

> Leave you feeling better about the situation and/or yourself.
> Can listen without telling you how to do it or what you should think.
> Have been through a similar experience and understand what you are talking about and how you feel.
> Encourage you to look deeper within yourself for your own answers.
> Don't think there is anything wrong with you because you feel this way.

If you read this list and draw a blank, realizing nobody you know fits this description, trust that there are people like this available, but you may have to look beyond your family and current circle of friends to find them. You may want to look for them as members of a support group related to your issue or try meeting this need through a helpful therapist or coach.

REFLECTION TWO: DON'T JUDGE YOUR REACTION, JUST HAVE IT

With some helpful support in your life, your next challenge is to stop evaluating how you're "handling" the situation. Just let yourself be. There is no one right way to react to a loss. You could cry; you could not cry at all. You could be angry or feel resentful. You could feel flat and empty. Or, you could see it as a larger part of the circle of life and quickly find peace for yourself. All of these, as well as an infinite array of other reactions, are perfectly appropriate.

Your reaction is just an extension of who you are, a representation of your feelings towards this situation and a vehicle for experiencing your own current reality. Expressing your true reaction can help you and others know what impact this loss is having on you. It also gives you and others some ideas on how to be the most supportive.

Some ways to turn your self-judgement off and make some room to just be and react are to:

> Make the following note for yourself, "However I grieve today, that is what is needed." Place this in an obvious place and allow it to remind you that, in each moment of the day, you can react in any way you choose.
> Stop and take a quiet moment to look at what restrictions you have placed upon yourself when you begin to feel

. bottled up inside.

➤ Spend some time alone every day if you find other people's presence inhibiting you. This will allow you the space you need to let your reactions come out.

➤ Tell those close to you that you are trying to let yourself react to the loss in whatever way you need to. That will both give you freedom to let it all hang out and help them to understand your various reactions.

➤ Read the following list of common reactions to loss at least once a week and remind yourself that feeling all of these things is very normal.

Ten Normal Reactions to Loss

1. Forgetfulness or missing appointments
2. Inability to concentrate or work
3. Crabby and irritable or dramatic mood changes
4. Appetite change, sudden weight gain or loss
5. Sleeplessness
6. Loss of interest or withdrawing from friends or activities you enjoyed before your loss
7. An overwhelming feeling of hopelessness, helplessness or despair
8. Fearing more losses and being overprotective of loved ones
9. Getting stuck trying to figure out the "whys"
10. Reliving or reassessing past losses

Through it all, remind yourself that stuffing your true feelings and reactions deep within yourself will only make it all more challenging in the long run. Let them come to the surface, experience them and then let them move out and make way for whatever is coming next.

REFLECTION THREE: DON'T TELL YOURSELF YOU SHOULD BE OVER IT, BE OVER IT WHEN YOU ARE OVER IT

Again, there is no right or wrong amount of time to be grieving a loss. There is nothing fast or predictable about working your way along the path of a loss. It is much more of a natural and organic process, needing time to take root, bear its fruit and then die back down. You don't want to let yourself get stuck in your grief and, in the process, miss all of life that is still before you or see yourself as forever victimized. But, at the same time, you cannot make yourself get over it if you are not over it. There is no switch to turn it all off. Trying to force your way through only seems to make the whole thing more confusing and lengthy. Instead, let yourself grieve when you feel the grief and simultaneously begin slowly putting the pieces of your life back together in some new form.

How do you know when you are beginning to force your way through your loss or, the flipside, allowing yourself to get stuck in it?

➤ If, when asked about the loss, you hear yourself saying, "I'm okay, I'm okay" and quickly move on to the next topic within a couple of days of experiencing your loss, you are likely rushing it.

➤ If you have told yourself it is not okay to have these emotions, and it is time to just get over it, you are likely forcing yourself through.

➤ If you have been relentlessly angry with yourself, another or God for over a month, you are probably beginning to get stuck.

➤ If you have been talking about it virtually nonstop for the past six months, you are likely getting stuck.

➤ If the loss is more than a year old, and you do not feel as if you have moved any further along in your grieving process, you still have the same intensity of feelings and emotions as you did in the first weeks of the loss, you are probably stuck in it.

On the other hand, if you are living your life, doing what needs to be done, feeling sorrow as well as a mix of other emotions such as joy, annoyance, contentment and pride, you are doing a great job of taking the time you need to attend to your loss without getting stuck in it.

Reflection Four: Forgive

Forgiveness is a wonderful rebirth that can come out of your loss. When you are ready, you will find it lifts your burdens and fills life with that beautiful brilliance you once knew so well. But like the whole process of living with loss, it cannot be forced or faked. You need some time to feel angry, bitter and hurt. Then, you can begin to see your openings for healing which are the true essence of forgiveness. What does it mean to open yourself up to forgiveness after being in a really tough spot? How do you know when you are ready to begin to forgive for all that has hurt you? You are ready:

> When you are open to being loved and cared for, as well as ready to give love and care to another.

> When you are willing to put yourself in a place where there is a chance you could be hurt by a similar incident again.

> When you find yourself aware of a reconnection to what matters most in life.

> When you are reminded that life is so short, and you know you need to take ahold of the present opportunity for resolution because it may be the last one you have.

> When you feel, in your heart, ready to accept all that a person brings, both the wonderful and the challenging. You now see you can appreciate the wonderful and deal in a loving way with the challenging.

This list can also be used as a map towards forgiveness. If forgiveness is a particularly hard place for you to find, use this list to begin to open yourself up to it. Begin by picking just one item from the list that you are ready to put back into your life. Commit to focus time each day on this single aspect of moving towards forgiveness. That may mean doing something to further the concept in your life, taking a quiet moment to look for where it is showing up in your day or stopping at the end of each day to appreciate how this initial step towards forgiveness has benefited you in some way throughout the day.

Now, reread those last two paragraphs with the realization that the person you may need to forgive the most is yourself. Is it time to stop blaming yourself, take yourself off the hook and accept you did the best you could do at the time? This can be some of the most challenging forgiveness to do. The could-have's and should-have's can make you crazy into eternity. They have pushed more than a few people into a pit of despair. Recognize you could not have, you should not have, you did your best at the time and set down the expectations that you had the power to make all this different. You just aren't quite that omnipotent. And if you did make a mistake, stop using it as a hammer with which to beat yourself and, instead, turn it into a lesson from which you can improve.

REFLECTION FIVE: DON'T BE SURPRISED IF IT SNEAKS IN AND YOU FEEL SAD AGAIN WHEN YOU THOUGHT YOU WERE OVER IT

You have looked bravely into the face of your loss, honestly felt the feelings that come with it, and begun to find your bearings. You are beginning to feel like the intense emotional sadness is really behind you. Then you are totally caught off guard when some common occurrence sparks those intense feelings back to life once again, as it likely will one day. Dee experienced this well after she thought she was over her miscarriage.

I remember my husband and I ran into a casual friend at the market about six weeks after my miscarriage. She was there with her new baby, whom we had heard was born but had not met yet. I took one look at her new baby and instantly felt a lump in my throat that began to rise. I choked out my congratulations and spent the rest of the day crying and missing my own baby who was gone. I remember being very surprised by the intensity of my pain. I thought I had gotten over all of that.

The pain of loss is funny in this way. It is as if it has a memory of its own. You think you have done your grieving, and then something you come across reawakens the intensity of that memory, and you are right back in the pain of that loss. But, this time, you have a new perspective on the emotion, and you don't feel quite as helpless or lost. Expect that your feelings will come and go. They are a natural part of the process and a valuable pearl to keep you in touch with what it means to be a human being.

REFLECTION SIX: FIND YOUR OWN MEANING IN THE LOSS

Finally, in moving further along in your process, you have the opportunity to see your loss from outside the pain and struggle to uncover what it has to teach you, what meaning you can take out of having gone through such an experience.

For many, this begins as a process of contemplating the whys. Why did this happen to me? Why did this happen to our baby? Why did our family have to go through this? The whys are such a natural place to begin looking for meaning, but there aren't usually many answers found in these pain-filled questions. Plain and simple, there probably is no answer to the whys of it all. It just happened.

What can be more helpful in uncovering your own meaning is

to shift your questioning beyond the whys and see how you have been altered by this experience. Some useful questions to ask are:

> How have your relationships been affected?
> What did you learn about yourself in getting through the loss?
> How do you see your life differently than you did prior to the loss?
> How have your priorities changed?
> Where have you felt the most pain through the loss?
> How do you now spend your time differently since the loss?
> How have you coped with the weight of the loss in your life?
> How have you gotten support and taken care of yourself through the loss?
> What does your future look like now that you have been through this loss?

The answers to these questions give you some threads of meaning. You can begin to weave this meaning together for yourself by sitting with those questions that jump out at you, doing some writing or just letting your mind toss them back and forth, and then seeing what awarenesses begin to come to the surface. You cannot force how or when these awarenesses come, but trust you will get something useful, and let it come when it is time.

A second, and very different approach to finding your own meaning in this loss is in taking actions that honor the connection you have to what has been lost. If you have had a miscarriage, this could mean taking some time to talk with others about the connection you have to the baby you carried. If you are experiencing a loss with your partner, this honoring could include stepping back and reminding yourself of the joys the two of you brought to one another prior to the loss. If your loss is in unfulfilled dreams of what your pregnancy, delivery or baby could have been, this honoring could begin by identifying the pieces of the experience that actually did fit your dreams. Some other specific actions you could take to honor your connection to what has been lost are to:

> Reconnect with your spiritual beliefs and take an action that is an extension of these beliefs. This could be reminding yourself again of forgiveness, recommitting to

the trust that you have in your higher power or adhering to your own religious customs when it comes to caring for your baby's body.

➢ Find an object which speaks to you about the loss. Let this object remind you of what is important in this situation, as well as honor the passage you have made by going through the fires of this loss.

➢ See the good in those around you and commit to spending time each day cherishing those people you have in your life.

➢ Keep your connection to this baby you cannot hold in your arms. You could do this by keeping out an ultrasound image or pictures of the baby, making a print of your baby's hand or foot, preserving a lock of hair, seeing her spirit alive in your life or remembering her birthday throughout the years.

➢ Create a celebration or rite of passage for yourself. This could be a baptism, a funeral, planting a tree or an acceptance ceremony. Include the other important people in your life as it suits you or the situation.

➢ Set up a structure so you intentionally revisit the loss over a period of time. This could be taking some time to write or read past writings every three months, going for a special walk alone once per month, thinking about how you have changed in relation to the loss or having coffee periodically with a friend with whom you can talk about the changes you experience around the loss.

➢ Create memories of your loss. This could be a special annual outing, keeping a journal, collecting pictures, or creating a reflective collage built of words, pictures or items from nature to move you along on your healing process. As the years go by, this can help to remind you of the details and impact of the loss, as well as celebrate the good that has come afterwards.

➢ Set up a memorial fund or a volunteer effort in the name or memory of the loss. Now, your loss can create good things in the lives of others.

All of these acts give you something to do and in the doing, you will find there will likely be some meaning that bubbles up for you. The meaning you find in either the questions you ask yourself or the acts you undertake to honor your connection can help bring some peace in a very painful time. Finding your own meaning doesn't take the pain away, but it does give you some strength, added insight and momentary emotional serenity, all of which can support you through this time and into your future. The meaning you find will aid you in moving from a place of isolated pain towards a reconnection to the larger world, opening insight into the pain of others and closer to the truth that life brings loss to us all. It is a part of living to stumble through that pain which we find in front of us. You are not alone.

Summary:
The True Emotions it Takes to Face a Pregnancy Loss

You have:

➤ Acceptance of yourself when you get choked up every time you read about, watch or participate in a pregnancy that reopens this loss.

➤ A remembrance of what it feels like to have lost something dear.

➤ A knowing that pregnancy loss is pain but it is pain tied to a love that is alive and creates a bond that will always connect you.

➤ The strength to allow a smile across your face when you still carry the burden of your pain.

➤ The courage to keep facing and working through the emotions of the moment rather than cutting yourself off from them.

➤ The willingness to allow yourself to trust, hold dear and finally love all over again.

The Unseen Strengths that Are Supporting You in Even the Worst Moments of Your Loss

You have:

➤ The concerns and prayers of your spouse, friends and family. Allow yourself to receive the care and support these people have to offer you.

➤ Your priorities. In everything you must go through, remember and act on those things that matter the most to you.

➤ Your inner strengths. You have more resilience, perseverance and patience than you may realize. Open yourself up to letting it all come out now.

➤ Your body. Use your physical reactions as a guide to work through the emotional reactions you are having.

➤ Your parental feelings. No matter what your loss, listen to these feelings, let them influence your actions and allow yourself to be the parent you have already become.

Resources

On Loss

Where Is God When It Hurts, Philip Yancey. (Grand Rapids, MI: Zondervan Publishing House, 2002.)

Life After Loss: A Personal Guide Dealing with Death, Divorce, Job Change and Relocation, Bob Deits. (Tucson, AZ: Fisher Books, 1999.)

The Grief Recovery Handbook: The Action Program for Moving Beyond Death, Divorce and Other Losses, John W. James and Russell Friedman. (New York, NY: HarperCollins, 1998.)

Good Grief Rituals: Tools for Healing: A Healing Companion, Elaine Childs-Gowell. (Station Hill Press, 1992.)

Good Grief: A Constructive Approach to the Problem of Loss, Granger E. Westberg. (Minneapolis, MN: Fortress Press, 1986.)

The Forum, Journal of ADEC, www.adec.org
The Association of Death Education and Counseling, Phone: 860-586-7503. Address: 638 Prospect Avenue, Hartford, CT 06105-4250.

On Pregnancy Loss

When a Baby Dies: The Experience of Late Miscarriage, Stillbirth and Neonatal Death, Nancy Kohner and Alix Henley. (New York, NY: Routledge, 2001.)

Trying Again: A Guide to Pregnancy After Miscarriage, Stillbirth and Infant Loss, Ann Douglas, John R. Sussman M..D. and Deborah Davis. (Dallas, TX: Taylor Publications, 2000.)

A Silent Sorrow Pregnancy Loss: Guidance and Support for You and Your Family, Ingrid Kohn, MSW, Lynn Moffitt Perry and Isabelle A. Wilkins M.D. (New York, NY: Routledge, 2000.)

A Broken Heart Still Beats: After Your Child Dies, Anne McCracken and Mary Semel. (Hazelden Information Education, 2000.)

From Sorrow to Serenity: Meditations for Those Who Have Suffered Pregnancy or Infant Loss, Susan Fletcher. (Alameda, CA: Hunter House, 1998.)

An Empty Cradle, a Full Heart: Reflections for Mothers and Fathers After Miscarriage, Stillbirth or Infant Death, Christine O'Keeffe Lafser and Phyllis Tickle. (Chicago, IL: Loyola Press, 1998.)

Mommy, Please Don't Cry, Linda Deymaz and Sabrina Smith. (Sisters, OR: Multnomah Publishers, 1997.)

Help, Comfort and Hope After Losing Your Baby in Pregnancy or the First Year, Hannah Lothrop. (Tucson, AZ: Fisher Books, 1997.)

Empty Cradle, Broken Heart: Surviving the Death of Your Baby, Deborah L. Davis Ph.D. (Golden, Colorado: Fulcrum Publishing, 1991 and 1996.)

Empty Arms: Coping with Miscarriage, Stillbirth and Infant Death, Sherokee Ilse, Edited by Arlene Applebaum. (Maple Plain, MN: Wintergreen Press, 1982, 1990, and 2000.)

Lifeline: A Journal for Parents Grieving a Miscarriage and Stillbirth, Pineapple Press, Phone: (517) 224-1881 PO Box 312, St. Johns, MI 48879.

Loving Arms, www.pilc.org
A quarterly newsletter of the Pregnancy and Infant Loss Center, Inc. Phone: (952) 473-9372 Address: 1421 E. Wayzata Blvd., Suite 70, Wayzata, MN 55391-1939.

AMEND, www.amendgroup.org
Aiding Mothers and Fathers Experiencing Neonatal Death. Call to get a list of services offered.
Phone: (314) 487-7582.
Address: c/o Maureen Connelly, 4324 Berrywick Terrace, St. Louis, MO 63128.

Pregnancy and Infant Loss Center, Inc., www.pilc.org
Publications, newsletter, cards, memory albums, video

cassettes and slide shows on prenatal bereavement, certificates of birth/baptism or blessing. Burial gowns. Call to get a mailing on the services offered from this organization.
Phone: (952) 473-9372.
Address: 1421 E. Wayzata Blvd., Suite 70, Wayzata, MN 55391-1939.

SHARE

Publications, newsletter, cards, memory albums, video cassettes and slide shows on prenatal bereavement, certificates of birth/baptism or blessing. Burial gowns. Call to get a mailing on the services offered from this organization.
Phone: (314) 947-6164 or (800) 821-6819.
Address: St. Joseph's Health Center, 300 First Capitol Drive, St. Charles, MO 63301-2893.

On Miscarriage

Silent Grief: Miscarriage — Finding Your Way Through the Darkness, Clara Hinton. (Greeenforest, AR: New Leaf Press, 1998.)

Our Stories of Miscarriage — Healing with Words, edited by Rachel Faldet and Karen Fitton. (Minneapolis, MN: Fairview Press, 1997.)

Miscarriage: Women Sharing from the Heart, Marie Allen, Ph.D. and Shelly Marks, MS. (New York, NY: John Wiley and Sons, 1993.)

Index

A

Christine D'Amico, MA provides coaching services to people in transition, including pregnancy, career issues and retirement. She received her Masters Degree in organizational change and adult education from the University of Minnesota in 1990 and has worked with concepts of change and personal development ever since. She lives in the upper midwest with her husband Dominic and their two young sons, with whom she has taken this amazing life-changing journey called pregnancy.

Margaret A. Taylor, MS, CNM has assisted more than one thousand women with the birth of their babies. She has been in practice since 1978 and has founded three midwife practices in the upper midwest. She is a Fellow of the American College of Nurse Midwives and is a leader in her profession. She lives in Plymouth, Minnesota, and spends her free time writing and enjoying her seventeen stepgrandchildren.

Order Coupon

To order additional copies of The Pregnant Woman's Companion, complete the order form below and mail to:

Attitude Press, Inc. P● Box 16095 Minneapolis, MN 55416 USA

The Pregnant Woman's Companion

Number of books: ____ at $14.95 for a total cost of $_____

Shipping and handling costs*: _____

Sales Tax of 6.5% for MN sales only: _____

Total Dollar amount due: _____ (Payable in US funds. No cash orders accepted).

*Shipping and handling: $2.50 for one book, $0.75 for each additional book, not to exceed $7.25

Enclosed is my: ___Check ____Money order

Please charge my ___Visa ____MasterCard ____American Express

Card #: _____

Expiration date: _____

Signature as on credit card: _____

Daytime phone number: _____

Ship to

Name: _____

Address: _____

City: _____ State: _____

Zip Code: _____

Please allow six weeks for delivery.
Prices subject to change without notice.